C000022118

1 MONTH OF
FREE
READING

at

www.ForgottenBooks.com

By purchasing this book you are eligible for one month membership to ForgottenBooks.com, giving you unlimited access to our entire collection of over 1,000,000 titles via our web site and mobile apps.

To claim your free month visit: www.forgottenbooks.com/free893045

* Offer is valid for 45 days from date of purchase. Terms and conditions apply.

ISBN 978-0-265-81108-5
PIBN 10893045

This book is a reproduction of an important historical work. Forgotten Books uses state-of-the-art technology to digitally reconstruct the work, preserving the original format whilst repairing imperfections present in the aged copy. In rare cases, an imperfection in the original, such as a blemish or missing page, may be replicated in our edition. We do, however, repair the vast majority of imperfections successfully; any imperfections that remain are intentionally left to preserve the state of such historical works.

Forgotten Books is a registered trademark of FB &c Ltd.
Copyright © 2018 FB &c Ltd.
FB &c Ltd, Dalton House, 60 Windsor Avenue, London, SW19 2RR.
Company number 08720141. Registered in England and Wales.

For support please visit www.forgottenbooks.com

FORTY-SEVENTH
ANNUAL REPORT

Hawaiian Mission
Children's Society

PRESENTED JUNE 3
1899

With Constitution and By-Laws
AND LIST OF MEMBERS

FORTY-SEVENTH

ANNUAL REPORT

OF THE

HAWAIIAN

Mission Children's Society

PRESENTED JUNE 3, 1899,

WITH THE

CONSTITUTION AND BY-LAWS:

AND LIST OF MEMBERS.

HONOLULU:
PRESS PUBLISHING COMPANY PRINT.
1899.

OFFICERS

FOR 1898-9.

REV. J. LEADINGHAM, President.

REV. A. V. SOARES, Vice-President.

REV. O. H. GULICK, Recording Secretary.

MARTHA A. CHAMBERLAIN and CHARLOTTE V. C. H
    Corresponding Secretaries.

LYLE A. DICKEY, Treasurer.

JOS. S. EMERSON and MRS. L. B. COAN, Elective Me
    of the Board.

OFFICERS

FOR 1899-1900.

A. FRANCIS COOKE, President.

FRANK C. ATHERTON, Vice-President.

LORRIN ANDREWS, Recording Secretary.

MARTHA A. CHAMBERLAIN and ADA WHITNEY, C
    ponding Secretaries.

LYLE A. DICKEY, Treasurer.

REV. J. LEADINGHAM and MRS. W. F. FREAR, El
    Members of the Board.

Minutes of Annual Meeting Held May 20, 1899.

Members of the Hawaiian Mission Children's Society gathered Saturday evening, May 20, for the annual meeting at the residence of Mr. A. F. Cooke, Rev. J. Leadingham, President, in the chair.

The meeting was opened by general singing and by prayer by Rev. O. P. Emerson.

The minutes of the last meeting were read and approved, and the report of the Board of Managers was also read.

The collection of the evening was......:...$22.05
Receipts from the sale of shells.......... 5.85
Receipts from life memberships.......... 10.00

Total................................$37.90

Committee for the preparation of a photographic album was appointed, consisting of Messrs. S. T. Alexander, Robert Andrews and O. H. Gulick.

By unanimous vote, Miss Kate Kelly was made eligible for membership.

The election of officers for the coming year resulted as follows:

President, A. F. Cooke; Vice President, Frank C. Atherton; Recording Secretary, Lorrin Andrews; Corresponding Secretaries, Miss M. A. Chamberlin, Miss Ada Whitney; Treasurer, Lyle A. Dickey; Elective Members of the Board, J. Leadingham, Mrs, W. F. Frear.

The appropriations for the current year, 1899–1900, were passed as follows:

Support of teachers in Kawaiahao Seminary..............$ 150
*Suppprt of pupils in Kawaiahao Seminary ....· 200
*Support of pupils in East Maui Female Seminary.......... 200
*Support of pupils in Kohala Girl's School................. 250

*Support of pupils in Hilo Boy's Boarding School.......... 200
Aid to schools of Chinese Misson.......... 200
Aid to Portuguese Mission work....................;.......... 200
Aid to Japanese Mission work................ 150
Aid to Mortlock teachers and evangelists................. 300
Aid to missionary on Pleasant Island..................... 100
Aid to the Hawaiian Board, a special gift for Mr Lutera,
   evangelist among the Gilbert Islanders in Lahaina........ 50
Aid to Gilbert Islands Mission work in the hands of Mr.
   Channon... 50
Corresponding Secretaries............................ . 100
Publishing Annual Report........... 110
Contingencies... 30

Total................................ ....$2290

A committee was chosen to provide music for the adjourned annual meeting and it was also voted that the lady of the house at which the meeting may be held shall have the privilege of providing the music.

Adjourned to meet for hearing the annual reports at the hall of Central Union Church June 3d, and closed with one verse of "From Greenland's Icy Mountains."

*Preference in the expenditure of this amount to be given to the children of Hawaiian missionaries and ministers.

Minutes of the Adjourned Annual Meeting.

The adjourned annual meeting of the Hawaiian Children's Society was held Saturday evening in the Sabbath School room of the Central Union Church. The principal business of the meeting was the reading of the annual reports by the retiring officers, and these were listened to with great interest by a large gathering.

The business of the meeting was pleasantly interspersed by the singing of a sextette of girls from the Portuguese Mission, girls of the Chinese Mission, and

Kawaiahao Seminary, the last named especially delighting their hearers.

Promptly at 7:30 the new President, A. F. Cooke, called the meeting to order, and after the completion of the routine business the little girls fron the Portuguese Mission. rendered a musical selection in their native tongue, which was much applauded.

Mr. O. H. Gulick, as Recording Secretary for the preceding year, next read his report, recapitulating the various meetings held and summarizing their results.

L. A. Dickey, as Treasurer, reported that after disbursing $2623 there was left in the treasury a balance of $589, with all obligations liquidated, affording, he added, a very cogent answer as to the Society's continued usefulness and the interest taken in it by its well wishers.

The scholars of the Chinese Mission then sang "Blow, Balmy Breath of Spring" in a way that reflected great credit upon themselves and their teachers.

Miss M. A. Chamberlain, as Corresponding Secretary, read an interesting paper chronicling the doings of the "cousins" in all parts of the world during the fiscal year, and was followed by an address by the retiring President, Rev. J. Leadingham, who chose for his subject, "Industrial Experiments in Hawaii and Their Influnces."

After a discussion of topics of interest by several members, and the singing of "Ring Out, Ye Bell" by the girls of the Kawaiahao Seminary, the meeting was declared adjourned.

It was one of the largest attended and most enthusiastic of the meetings held for some time by the Society, and proved conclusively, as one member put it, that "the flame which kindled the Society, still burns brightly in the hearts of its present members."

LORRIN ANDREWS,
Recording Secretary.

Annual Report of Recording Secretary.

The monthly meetings have been held throughout the year, a part of the time on Friday evenings, but usually on Saturday evenings.

Two families have entertained the Society twice during the year, and seven once. Two meetings have been held on Nuuanu street, two on Punahou street, while seven have been held in what might be called Central Honolulu.

Those who attend the Society meetings are largely the older men and women of the cousinhood, those whose interest was enlisted in the days of their youth, and when the Society organization itself was young.

Our meetings constitute a point of attraction to those visitors coming to our city whose interest is alive to missionary history. While there is no systematic pursuit of island or missionary history, yet at our meetings very frequently matters of great interest from both a missionary and historical point of view are brought forward. For those cousins who would keep in touch with the unique conditions of life and lore in these Islands, the meetings of our Society are of great value. At no small proportion of our meetings some passing missionary or some special friend of the missionary cause, or some aquaintance of some of the missionary fathers is present as a visitor for the evening. At some of our meetings we have had present several foreign missionaries passing from the Continent of America to Asia, or returning from the Eastern to the Western Continent. More and more is the Society becoming a breathing place for some of the earnest missionary spirits in this community. While we are not by any means the sole depositaries of the missionary spirit in these Islands, we are one of the agencies that help to keep alive the missionary traditions and purposes that have had so wonderful a part in shaping the well-being of our island community.

While a portion of those coming to our shores see

nothing in this land but an arena upon which to exploit their personal fortunes, there are those to whom life and country is something else, something more than a fortune or even than mere bread and butter.

The increasing interest of this Society in the missionary field around us, and beyond us, is a token of future usefulness which may well lead us to look hopefully foreward.

A glance at some of the topics that have engaged the thought of this Society during the past year will be of interest. Among these may be mentioned Mr. and Mrs. Philip de la Porte and their mission to Pleasant Island, towards whose support this Society contributes; Mrs. McCully Higgins' account of the men who have been judges of the Supreme Court of Hawaii for the past fifty years; the loss by fire of the Maunalua Seminary of East Maui, and the expectation of its early restoration; the furnishing of country libraries and reading rooms for the needy communities of our land and people; portions of Hawaiian history and folk lore, from Mrs. Joseph Emerson's facile pen; Miss Aikue's accurate and able essay upon the missiontry field of Micronesia; the comparison of Christian Science with the theosophy of India, by Pundita Ramabai; a thoughtful view of the present condition of the Hawaiian churches and native Christians, by Miss M. A. Chamberlain; an interesting portion of a journal to one of our honored missionary fathers, written on the Cape Horn voyage, and read by justice Judd; thrilling reminiscences of the eruption of Mauna Loa, in 1880, which threatened the destruction of Hilo town and harbor, by Mrs. L. B. Coan, an eye witness; the work of Boy's Clubs and the need of such work, set forth by Mr. Pond and Professor Richards; an interesting account by Professor W. D. Alexander of a visit to Neblous, the ancient Schecheme, home of the few remaining Samaritans; an able essay by Dr. S. E. Bishop, entitled "America and the Philippines;" Thomas Gulick's account of the midnight sun seen in the Arctic zone on the shores of Spitzbergen, in 1898.

Besides these we have had brief, but valuable missionary talks from Mrs. Sheffield and Dr. John Gulick, of China and Japan respectively.

And still further may be mentioned brief extracts read from letters of absent cousins, among whom are to be found some of the most brilliant letter writers of this or any age, such as Professor A. B. Lyons and his gifted daughter.

A Society which in a twelvemonth presents such a panorama of life in these halcyon Islands, besides raising $2200 for home and foreign missionary purposes, and which constitutes the link that binds together a thousand cousins scattered in every quarter of the globe, is not to be despised, or its existence to be apologized for.

The cousin who can afford to forego both the pleasure and the profit of such a course of instructive and inspiring experience as this Society affords, must be both rich in resources and happy indeed in private springs of inspiration.

O. H. GULICK,
Recording Secretary.

Honolulu, June 3, 1899.

Corresponding Secretary's Report.

As our last year's Report closed, we stood gazing in surprise and wonder at the events of history which were rapidly unfolding before our eyes. The months of June, July and August were memorable indeed. The constant arrival of volunteer U. S. troops bound for the Philippines ; the entertaining and helping these thousands of young men in their few days of rest in Hawaii nei, while in transit, absorbed the time, thought and energy of nearly all the residents of Honolulu, in all which scenes and labors the members of this Society held active participation.

A Red Cross Society was early formed by the ladies, which soon had abundant call for action and sympathy. Annexation, which had for five years hung in the balance in the deliberations at Washington, D. C., became a war necessity. The joint resolution for the annexation of Hawaii passed the House of Representatives June 18th by a vote of 209 to 91. It was immediately taken up by the Senate, where, after a protracted debate, the final passage was carried July 6th by a vote of 42 to 21, and was signed by President McKinley July 7th. The final news of annexation was brought to Honolulu by the Coptic, on the morning of July 13th. A salute of one hundred guns was fired, and the announcement was received with great demonstrations of joy, especially by all who claimed allegiance to the United States of America, although to many a Hawaiian-born subject of the United States sorrow mingled with the joy that day.

It was however a full month after the news had been received, that the long looked for event of Flag Raising took place, and Hawaii became part of the United States of America.

No better account can be given of the emotions of that occasion than a quotation from the pen of our cousin, Rev. S. E. Bishop, in the Friend for September:

"As the time drew near for the official transfer of sovereignty, the thought of making the day one of great public rejoicing gradually gave way to a due appreciation of the solemnity of the occasion, and led the people to fully commend the decision   *   *   * to confine it to a strictly official ceremony of democratic simplicity. Not only did memories and sentiment crowd all joyous thought from mind, as the Hawaiian flag was lowered, and our band played the national anthem, 'Hawaii Ponoi,' but it modified the volume of cheer that greeted 'Old Glory' as it rose in its place to the strains of the 'Star Spangled Banner' by the Philadelphia's band. In place of the cheers which many expected to give, they found themselves subject to emotions which dimmed not a few eyes with tears ; not that they regretted to see the 'emblem of the free' borne on the breeze as the flag of this land, with the feeling of security it assured to all, and its guarantee of material prosperity, but, as it were, a passing sigh for what 'might have been.' "

In the numerous photographs of the scenes taken that day, the faithful *sunshine* has impressed for all posterity, the *shadow* that fell on a thousand hearts.

The war with Spain was practically ended by the grand naval victories in Cuba early in July, and peace was declared about the same time that the annexation of Hawaii became a fixed fact. But the effects of the war with Spain on our missions in the Caroline group were not overcome by the joyful news of peace. The hope we had ardently cherished that one of the U. S. warships might be ordered to take possession of Ponape, on the way down to Manila, was not realized. Although Guam was taken, the much more valuable Carolines were neglected, and were therefore left in the hands of Spain, on the formal conclusion of the treaty of peace.

It was not deemed safe to send the "Morning Star" on her usual trip in June. One of the early events of the year affecting our missionary work was the brief visit of a few hours of Dr. Judson Smith, the senior Secretary of the A. B. C. F. M., who touched at Hon olulu June 29th, on his return from an official tour in visiting the missions of the Board in China. The officers of the Hawaiian Board were able to hold a short conference with him, which was most highly prized, in which the affairs of the Micronesia Mission and movements of the "Morning Star" were discussed and decision made. After his return to the Mainland, orders were sent out from Boston that the "Morning Star" be sent over to San Francisco to remain until early in 1899, and she left for that port the first week in August. Capt. Bray and his family went over with her. A schooner, "Queen of the Isles," was chartered in San Francisco in August, and departed with the mail and needed supplies for the missionaries waiting in suspense on those lonely isles. She took as passengers Rev. and Mrs. Channon and four children, returning to Kusaie; and Rev. M. L. Stimson and the Misses Elizabeth and Jane Baldwin, all new helpers bound for Ruk.

Here we quote a few extracts from Mrs. Logan's journal to picture the Micronesia side of this year:

"Thanksgiving Day, Nov. 24th, 1898.—We have been more completely shut off from communication with the outside world than usual. Captain Melander, who usually comes to us once in four or five months, and at least brings us news from friends in Kusaie, has not been here since March. He came once as near as Losap, and left a short letter there for Mr. Price, saying he was forbidden to come to Ruk by the Spanish government, and also forbidden to tell the reason why, but that we would learn about it before very long. A Japanese trading schooner brought us mail and told us that there was war between the United States and Spain. Further than this we had no news, save that word finally came from Ponape, that when Capt. Me lander returned to Ponape his vessel was taken by the Spaniards and he was made a prisoner. Also that Henry Nanpei was in prison, and it was feared that the Spaniards would kill him. * * We closed school August 1st, hoping to see the 'Star' before we should begin another year; but when she had not come early in September, we began again, because it is necessary to keep our scholars fairly busy.

"The days passed away, and we finished a term of six weeks, and still no 'Star;' and no word from any-where. We began to have a real shut—in feeling. Surely, something was happening somewhere in the great world. Were there stirring events of which we knew nothing? Who could tell? Had our 'Morning Star' been captured by the Spanish at Kusaie? In that case when would we ever get our mail? What should we do for supplies? One sunrise was as good as another, and there was nothing to do but wait, and that as patiently as possible. Our supplies were holding out fairly well, although Mr. Price said he did not know but we should be ready to adopt the form of blessing used by some poor College students who boarded themselves, 'O Lord we thank Thee for this miserable food provided for our dying bodies.' * * * * Then, very early one morning, as soon as it was light enough to see,—it was the morning of November 8th —there was a rushing of natives past the house, out to the brow of the hill where there is a good view of the sea. To the eager inquiry, 'What is the matter?' there came the equally eager reply, 'There is a ship in sight !' I hurried out with the glass. Not the 'Morn ing Star,' surely; only a schooner. The Japs are looking for one of their vessels ; probably this is it. Well, we may get some letters. Later it is plain from the rig that it is not a Japanese schooner. Now she is inside the lagoon, and seemed to to be heading for our station ; indeed, her nose seemed to be pointing directly on to our front door. Mr. Price and Captain Foster have gone to Fairuk, out to the west part of the lagoon, ten or fifteen miles away, and they have both boats with them. What is to be done? We can send one of the native boys off in a canoe, but we are eager for mail, and fear we should get little in that way. So Beulah and Mrs. Foster rise to the occasion, send and get Mr. Coe's boat (he is a respecfable trader who goes as mate on the Logan) and are off for news about the time the vessel comes to anchor. Missionaries! Mail ! Supplies ! Oh ! how much it means to us ! The dear friends who have come to help us have had a cramped, weary, seasick voyage of seventy-four days, but they have reached us at last ! Does any one say we do not get some glimpse of heavenly joys here on

earth? Let him come and be a missonary in Micronesia. We can assure him of joyful experiences, as
well as those which are supposed to develop saintliness.
Friends, letters, food, potatoes, onions—even apples!
War! Victory! Annexation! How things do crowd
together and tumble over each other! We have
hardly caught our breath yet, though many days have
slipped away."

It was in the month of August that the depressing
news reached Honolulu of Henry Nanpei's imprison-
ment with all his family by the Spanish garrison. No
reason was given for this high-handed attack, "excepting that Mr. Nanpei is a Protestant, and will not
abjure his faith for that of the Roman Catholic Church,
and has, as native Govenor of the Islands, used all his
influence toward the maintainance of the churches and
schools established by the American Protestant missionaries."

By a chance vessel that arrived in San Francisco
April 23, with later news, Mr. Nanpei was still in
prison. His life does not seem to be in danger, but he
is kept as hostage by the Spaniards. A most disás-
trous hurricane had been experienced at Kusaie.
There are tribal wars raging in Ruk. We shall long
for particulars by return of the "Morning Star."

Our missionary vessel returned from San Francisco March 23d, 1899, and was dispatched on her west-
ward cruise April 7th. It has been decided to change
the time of the annual start to the earlier months of
the year, to avoid adverse winds and currents which it
has been proved,retard the trips of the missionary vessel when she starts in June or July. She took with
her to further reinforce the Missions, Mrs. L. C. Stim-.
son going with three children to join the father in
Ruk, Miss Louise Wilson, of Kusaie, returning from
her furlough; Mr. and Mrs. De la Porte, German-
American helpers bound for Pleasant Island, which is
under German control and has never yet had a missionary. This couple of devoted Christian laborers

came to Honolulu last June, expecting to take imme-
diate passage in the "Morning Star." The Hawaiian
Mission Children's Society has appropriated $100
toward their support, and other contributions were
made by the Central Union Church and individuals.
They are not under the control of the A. B. C. F. M.
It was a pleasure and inspiration to become acquainted
with these humble consecrated helpers. A little daughter who was given them during their stay here, was
baptised in Central Union Church, which fellowship the
parents entered while here, so they now belong to us
in a special way of love.

Capt. Bray resigned command of the "Morning
Star" after he had brought her back from San Francisco, and Capt. Garland again took this part of missionary service. Mrs. Garland and their two little girls
accompanied him.

We must not leave our record of Micronesia items
without mention of the brief call of Rev. F. M. Price,
in one of the China steamers, March 10th. He came
via Japan and was on his way home for medical treat-
ment. He brought the news of the wreck of the R.
W. Logan at Satoan, in a most unusual westerly gale,
while she was on a missionary tour through the Mort-
locks. Mr. Price and Miss Beulah Logan had a nar-
row escape with their lives. Mrs. Logan's journal
gives the account of the trip, but our limits forbid further extracts. A late item connected with Micronesia
is clipped from a San Francisco paper which tells of
the arrival of the little craft : " 'Hiram Bingham,' after
a perilous voyage, which Rev. Mr. Walkup undertook
to carry a company of shipwrecked sailors back. The
sails were torn to pieces and replaced by gunny bag
sails. Starvation stared them in the face, but they
were delivered."

War and Missions seem intertwined in our record
this year. We feel this, as we write of Spain and re-
call the interesting account of our missionary cousin,
Wm. H. Gulick, last year, in the removal of their Girls'

School over the border into France. We have heard a rumor that the school was to be transferred again to Spain and be reopened in Madrid. Mrs. Wm. H. G. has returned to Spain, after an absence of several years, with restored health, and having secured, by personal efforts, a handsome sum of money towards the building of a permanent institution. She is now warmly enlisted in the plan of the Madrid settlement. Two highly educated and consecrated young ladies returned with her as helpers, who go on their own means. Since this Report was finished a letter has arrived from Rev. Wm. H. Gulick, which tells of their successful year in Biarritz.

Japan has sent us no letter this year, but we have met our cousins, Rev. and Mrs. John T. Gulick and their daughter Louise, who is accompanied by another young lady, daughter of one of their Japan missionary associates. They arrived early in April and are still with us. They are on a trip to the United States for rest, and plan to remain until after our June anniversaries. It has been a great pleasure to meet them and hear their reports of work in Japan given at various meetings. More and more is the trip to Japan becoming popular with the cousins. This spring Mrs. J. B. Atherton and daughter Mrs. Theodore Richards, and Miss Grace Cooke. with Mr. and Mrs. F. J. Lowrey, and Mr. and Mrs. George Carter, have all taken the tour, and we expect a reflex influence of missionary zeal on their return.

Our Missionary Record will not be complete without the mention of the arrival of the venerable Rev. James Kekela from the Marquesas Is., with his family of children and grandchildren to the number of fourteen, on the 5th of April. For many years this Society paid a portion of their appropriation to the Marquesas Mission, and received personal letters from Revs. J. Kekela and S. Kauwealoha. The noble wife, Mrs. Naomi Kekela, has never before returned to her native land since she entered missionary service in 1853—

forty six years ago—leaving behind her an infant daughter, (scarce three years old) Maria Ogden Ke-kela, as the adopted child of her beloved "teacher-mother," Miss Maria Ogden. It was Mrs. Maria K. Martyn's sweet pleasure to receive and make a home in Honolulu for them on their return. Many of their grandchildren will now be put into the fine boarding schools here. Three of Kekela's daughters have been previously educated and settled here. Two more of the daughters have had education in the French Protestant schools of Tahiti and speak nothing but French. Both have taught in French in the Government schools at the Marquesas. Rev. S Kauwealoha, who remains at Fatuhiwa, never had any children, but adopted one of Mr. Kekela's sons, and some of his children are among these grandchildren. Our Society has voted to give part of their appropriations this year to these children.

The Armenian orphans, for whom our cousin Mrs. Fannie (Andrews) Shepard has so ardently awakened the sympathies of Mrs. A. F. Judd, have been, through Mrs. Judd's appeals, most generously aided by extra contributions from the ladies of the W. B. M. P. I.

It would be interesting if we could note all those of this Society who have been participators in this war with Spain. We know of them but partially, but mention that Lieut. Theodore F. Forbes did very responsible duty for months in Florida, in drilling and and preparing troops for the Cuban campaign, and expected daily to be sent himself, but the war closed before his services were called for outside the main-land. Dr. James B. Judd was actively engaged in all the Cuban campaign as a surgeon, and his letters home were of intense interest. Many extracts from them were shared with his numerous friends here. Alfred Dole, at Manila, has been in many a battle, but so far has escaped unharmed by bullet or sickness. His let-ters have been published in our local papers.

A letter from Rev. Horace J. Taylor, once a missionary at Apaiang, Micronesia, has been read at a Society meeting, telling of his son Semour (whom some of us remember as a frail infant of two years going down to Micronesia with his parents, and later returning motherless) having as a stalwart young man, enlisted last spring as a volunteer in the war with Spain. His duty was assigned at Camp Alger, and in that camp of notorious sickness and death, he escaped the least shadow of illness and did grand duty, owing to his strict observance of all the laws of health.

The following clipping was found in a copy of the Advance near the close of 1898:

"The annexation of Hawaii is already bearing fruit, for at a recent convocation President Harper announced a contribution of fifteen hundred dollars by the Castle family, of Hawaii, to the University of Chicago."

GENERAL CORRESPONDENCE.

It gives us much pleasure to record a number of acknowledgments of the last Annual Report with messages of aloha to the Society. Among these, first, we note a letter from Mrs. Alice (Thurston) Stevenson, of Taylorsville, N. C., who sent a fine photograph of Asa Thurston 3rd, her son by our lamented cousin, Rev. Thomas G. Thurston. He is now a youth preparing for College. His sister Lucy is completing her third year in the Greensboro Normal College, N. C. Words of appreciation on receiving the Report from Mrs. Prudence (Winter) Kofoid, Miss Helen S. Norton, Miss N. writes with her "aloha nui" to the Society, "I esteem it a great privilege to be counted a 'cousin' by such a band. Letters from Miss L. F. Ingraham, Miss Helen E. Carpenter, Rev. James P. Chamberlain, Mary E. Goodale and Joel Bean were welcome.

The letter of Joel Bean, of San Jose, Cal., mentioned that their youngest daughter, Catherine Cox, with her husband Isaac Cox, and little son, were soon to be residents of Maui, where his son-in-law was engaged as tutor in the family of a resident of Waihee. He hoped "Cathie" might be welcomed as a "cousin." The Secretary soon wrote her a note of welcome, and received a charming reply.

A letter from Rev. Claude Severance, once a teacher at Oahu College, and later missionary in Japan, where he married a missionary teacher, Miss Almona Gill, gives particulars of the death of his wife. They were obliged to leave Japan on account of the failure of her health, but had been settled in Cleveland O., two years and had founded a Mission Church, which from humble start had grown into a prosperous community, and had erected a pretty chapel. He sent an illustrated pamphlet of the service of dedication on December 4, 1898. His dear wife, who had helped so much to organize the church, died November 7th, a month previous. Mr. Severence is deeply interested in the Japanese work, and queries if there might not be some position for him in this same work in Hawaii A letter from Mr. S. T. Alexander, dated New Years Day, 1899, introduced a subject very near his heart, namely, "the inaugurat ing of a movement towards the securing of the like-nesses of all the old missionary fathers and mothers who have lived, or still live, on these islands." As this subject was taken up at the January Cousins' Meeting, and a committee appointed to report at a future time, and as this report of the committee is to be published and circulated this year, in our booklet, we bespeak a very careful reading of the subject and expression of approval by subscriptions. Of course *replies* are expected.

Our own Education work has been diligently per— formed this year, and the reports sent in are full of in-terest. They will be printed in full. We bespeak a very careful reading of them.

Miss M. E. Alexander, of the Maunaolu Seminary, at Makawao, has given so few particulars of the fire in September that we must give a little more of that history. It was in September, a few weeks after the re-opening of the fall term. The fire seems to have started in the attic from some cause unknown, and the wind being high, and *no water* accessible, the building was soon reduced to ashes and a total loss, nothing being saved but the new *piano*, a very late gift from Mrs. H. P. Baldwin. It was a great cause for thankfulness that it was early, before any of the girls had retired, and no lives were lost. The sympathy of the entire Island community was enlisted at once. Large and generous contributions of clothes, money and all sorts of articles were sent in at once in Honolulu, at the call of Mr. W. W. Hall, who packed and sent the boxes with the utmost dispatch. All the other island communities responded. The old Makawo church sheltered the homeless ones that night and for some succeeding days, until the quarters on the Haleakela Ranch could be secured. The old building on Mrs. Helen T. Alexander's property that was once used for the Boys' Farm School, has been utilized this year. Within a week after the destruction of the old building, Hon. Henry P. Baldwin announced his intention to *rebuild* the Seminary, all the expense beyond the partial insurance to be assumed by himself. This filled all the hearts of teachers, pupils and friends with gratitude and love. The plans have just been secured and the contracts called for. Whether the building will be completed before the usual time of the opening next fall is not certain. It was at once decided not to rebuild on the old site, where water is so perilously scarce. "Sunnyside," Paiia, is Mr. Baldwin's own choice, his own property.

In speaking of education, a few words concerning Kamehameha Schools seem called for. Since the opening of these successful and finely equipped institutions founded by Mrs. Bernice P. Bishop, eleven years have passed, and the results have seemed magical. In all these years—though often severe illness has enter ed—there had never been a death until this year.

Joseph Nabele, of Kona, a member of the graduating class which is to go out this month, died last week, after a swift run of fever. He has been in the school a trusted and beloved pupil from the Preparatory department up. His body was embalmed and after a week sent home for interment. On the morning of May 30th, Decoration Day, a most touching and beautiful service was held in the Chapel, beginning at 8 a. m. The sunlight, streaming through the stained glass window that faces the east, fell on the flower-covered casket, making the place full of brightness and not of gloom. The three companies that came in from the three schools—first the girls in white, then the little boys, also in white, with black neckties, and last, the different classes of the boys from the Kamehameha Manual, all in the school uniform, made an impressive picture. The services were tender and appropriate : Scripture reading by Mr. Perry, the school chaplain ; a prayer in Hawaiian from Rev. Mr. Timoteo ; lovely and heart-filled songs from both the girls' and boys' departments; and finally the most appropriate and inspiring short sermon from Mr. Theodore Richards, the late Principal, made a most impressive service. And the last act, the procession of the entire boys' department passing around the casket, each laying a flower as he passed somewhere upon the other floral decorations, was one to fill all eyes with tears. Then reverently and tenderly, his classmates who were the pallbearers and dressed in mourning, lifted the casket on their shoulders and bore him out from the sacred place. Only the boys of the Manual department marched in the procession to the wharf, headed by their own band. Mr. Richards' work for this beloved school is by no means ended by his resignation. A large and far–reaching work for all the graduates is quietly going on, and his efforts in the Union Sabbath School work, training the teachers in *all* the various schools of the city, are showing fruitage already. A magnificent Sunday School Rally was

held on May 13th, of which our limits forbid any en-
larged account.

The efficient and highly appreciated efforts of Mr.
Hiram Bingham, Jr., for six months in the Palama
Chapel, make us regret to record that he has sent in
his resignation, as the strain seriously affected his
health. He went for recuperation to Molokai, where
he has found some employment while he is resting
from excitement. Just before he left Honolulu Mr.
Bingham gave a very delightful Reception and After-
noon Tea in his parents' home, March 8th, to over two
hundred friends, in honor of the seventieth birth-
day of his aunt, Miss E. K. Bingham. Friends entered warmly into the occasion, and a purse of over
one hundred dollars was given her, which came as a
complete surprise. Many other beautiful gifts were
brought.

The departure of Rev. and Mrs. C. M. Hyde for San
Francisco, on the 13th of May, caused deep regret,
since Dr. Hyde's health is delicate. But he had so
strong a desire to take the trip and visit his son in
Ware, Mass., with hope that a change of climate
might recuperate him, his devoted wife gained courage
to attempt it. We have heard of his safe arrival in
San Francisco, with some improvement on the passage, and they were to start east about May 27th.

Central Union Church welcomed to its pastorate in
September, 1898, Rev. Wm. M. Kincaid, a worthy
successor to the line of able pastors we have already
enjoyed. He has quickly secured the hearts of the
community, and it is a pleasing feature of every evening service to see the numbers of young people. The
youth of the Hawaiian and Chinese boarding schools
are often present, and lately chorus singing by the
girls of the Kamehameha and Kawaiahao Schools has
been an attractive feature of the service.

Rev. J. A. Cruzan is settled in Hilo, doing grand
work, and Rev. C. W. Hill has a growing influence as
Home Mission pastor in Olaa and Kau.

MARRIAGES.

We head this list with one that should have been entered in last year's Report, but has only very lately been reported.

In Bay City, Michigan, April 11, 1898, Mr. William Lee Bond to Miss Laura Belle Lewis.

In Honolulu, at the Portuguese Church, by Rev. C. M. Hyde, July 7th, 1898, Rev. A. V. Soares to Miss Arcenia Fernandes.

In Honolulu, August 11, '98, Mr. Clarence Hyde Cooke to Miss Lily Love.

At Haiku, Maui, August 20, '98, Mr. Duncan B. Murdock to Miss Mary Eames Baldwin.

In Oakland, Cal., September 30, '98, Mr. Frederick Burke to Miss Caroline Frear.

At Colorado Springs, Col., Oct. 26, '98, Mr. Paul F. De la Vergne to Miss Clara C. Kennedy.

At Haiku, Maui, Nov. 23, '98, Mr. Henry Waterhouse, Jr., to Miss Grace Graydon Dickey.

In Honolulu, Dec. 20, '98, Dr. Wm. L. Moore, of Hilo, to Miss Ellen Moore Lowrey.

In New York City, Dec. 27th, 1898, Mr. Lorrin Andrews to Miss Estelle Linwood.

In Central Union Church, Honolulu, Jan. 12th, 1899, Mr. Walter L. Howard to Mrs. Margaret Hare Goddard.

In Glasgow, Scotland, Jan. 17th, 1899, Mr. Samuel Edward Damon, of Honolulu, to Miss Gertrude McKinnon.

In New York City, April 5th, 1899, Dr. Charles E. Davis to Mrs. Mary Scott–Carter, widow of Charles L. Carter, of Honolulu.

In Honolulu, April 21, '99, at the Kamehameha Chapel, Mr. W. W. Bristol to Miss Olive Lamb. Mr. B. is a teacher in the school and Miss Lamb came on from the States to join him.

In Honolulu, May 25, '99, at the home of her brother, Wm. O. Smith, Miss Juliette Smith, of Koloa, Kauai, to Mr. J. K. Farley, also a resident of Koloa for many years.

In Honolulu, May 24, '99, Philip L.Weaver to Miss Agnes Crary, of San Jose, Cal. Mr. Weaver is the son of Ellen (Armstrong) Weaver.

In Honolulu, at the N. Pacific Missionary Institute, May 16, '99, Mr. Horace J. Craft to Miss Helen K. Wilder.

Honolulu, June 20, 1899.—As our Report is in press, we still chronicle for this year one more marriage: Mr. Charles Atwood Rice of Lihue and Miss Grace Ethel King, of Honolulu.

BIRTHS.

In Hilo, July 11th, 1898, to Mrs. Levi C. Lyman, a daughter, Katheryne Isobel.

*In Evanston, Ill., August 13, '98, to Mrs. Caroline (Clark) Balding, a daughter.

In Honolulu, August, 1898, to Mrs.Frances(Kinney) Dickey, a son, Herbert Alexander.

In Honolulu, Aug., 1898, to Mrs. S. G.Wilder, a son.

In Chicago, Ill., Oct. 9th, 1898, to Mrs. Walter S. Dole, a son.

In Honolulu, October 10, 1898, to Mrs. Wm. O. At-water, twin sons, Curtis and Benner.

In Boston, Mass., November 8th, 1898, to Mrs. Emma (Whitney) Goodale, a son, Holbrook Marsh.

In Columbus, Ohio, November, 1898, to Mrs. Helen (Dickson) Pratt, a son, Howard Dickson.

In Japan, December, 1898, to Mrs. Sidney L. Gu-lick, a daughter, Ethel.

In Philadelphia, Pa., Dec. 13, 1898, to Mrs. Ada (Jones) Gartley, a daughter, Ruth.

In Wailuku, Maui, January, '1899, to Mrs. J. M. Lewis, a daughter.

In Honolulu, February 5th, 1899, to Mrs. Eleanor (Sisson) Thrum, a daughter, Eleanor Sisson.

---

*Mr. and Mrs. Baldwin are now residents of Hawaii, having lived at Wainaku, Hilo, since November, 1898.

In Hilo, February 8th, 1899, to Mrs. Grace L. (Wing) Crockett, a son.

In Honolulu, February 13th, 1899, to Mrs. Mildred (Kinney) Wells, a son, George Herbert.

In Honolulu, March 14th, 1899, to Mrs. Herbert A. Austin, a daughter.

In Honolulu, March 26th, 1899, to Mrs. D. Howard Hitchcock, a son, Howard Harvey.

In Hilo, May, 1899, to Mrs. R. K. Baptiste, a son.

In Kohala, May 10, '99, to Mrs. Dr. B. D. Bond, a son.

DEATHS.

At Waikane, Oahu, on Sabbath morning, July 7th, 1898, died of pneumonia, Edwin Austin Jones. His remains were brought home to Honolulu. A shadow of bereavement fell on the community, for in his home, in business, in the church and the Y. M. C. A., though never making any display of himself, he had been a staff to lean on, a light not hid.

At Lihue, Kauai, July 23d, after a lingering decline from consumption, Miss Mary H. Hardy entered upon rest, aged 37 years.

At Kohala, Hawaii, October 9th, 1898, Edward G. Hitchcock ended his brave life. For eight months he had been a great sufferer from the effects of a carbuncle on the back of the neck. It was only his indomitable will and pluck, that led him to persist in going to preside as Judge at the Circuit Court. He succumbed at once to weakness and died in three days. His remains were sent back to Hilo, and his funeral was held in the Haili Church.

Died in Washington, D. C., at the age of 62, Philip Inch, husband of Clara Dibble, the youngest child of Sheldon Dibble, formerly a missionary here and the Hawaiian historian. Mr. Inch held high position as Lieutenant of Engineers in the U. S. N., and had often visited Honolulu, where he was always glad to claim his cousinship. He was much esteemed in the church to which he belonged in Washington, and a copy of his funeral discourse was sent to Prof. W. D. Alexander by his pastor.

At Haiku, Maui, November 23d, the very evening when Maui society was met to greet the wedding bells of two cousins of the second generation, the sweet and saintly soul of Geo. E. Beckwith was peacefully passing over the bar into the sea of eternity, after a brief illness. His brother, Rev. Edward G. Beckwith, went from the death scene to perform the happy ceremony, nor did he suffer one look or word to mar his serenity. He knew his brother would have wished no shadow to go from him to the home of his neighbors of many years. The next day all Maui met at Paiia church in mourning over their great loss. The two daughters of Mrs. Geo. E. Beckwith, who were both teaching in the United States, returned as swiftly as it was possible to comfort their mother. But now the lovely home at Haiku is broken up, Mrs. Beckwith and daughters having returned to the United States to reside.

Died, in Saybrook, Conn., Mrs. Emily (Whitney) McCall. She was the youngest daughter of the pioneer missionaries, Rev. Samuel and Mrs. Mercy P. Whitney.

On the early morning of January 15th, 1899, the Messenger came for our beloved Sarah (Andrews) Thurston, who had lingered a month paralyzed and unable to communicate her thoughts or feelings. She, whose mature history was bound up in that of the Hawaiian Mission Children's Society for forty—six and a half years, since she was the first Vice President of this Society ; and her husband, Asa Thurston, delivered the first President's address. In the third year of our organization they joined *wedded hands* "till death do us part." The parting came in the year 1859, and she walked amidst us a widow for forty years. Three small children were left to rear and educate on very small means. Her character can be written in three short words : sweet, sunny, strong—else how could she ever have horne such burdens. When Robert, her eldest son, had just reached manhood, he was taken from her by a sudden casualty, yet no murmer was ever uttered. No shadow from her life was ever permitted to darken another's. Later years lightened her toils, but her deeds of helpfulness never ceased. In the old Andrews homestead, in Nuuanu, we met around her peaceful form, and she was borne from its shadow by the hands of "Cousins," to be laid in the last rest. The procession walked down the hill to the grave, and another link to the past was severed.

Under a mental cloud, caused by disease and mental suffering, Henry H. Wilcox closed his life prematurely, January 11th, 1899.

> We see but dimly through the mists and vapors
> Amid these earthly damps ;
> What seem to us but sad funereal tapers
> May be heaven's distant lamps.

The death of three little ones must be recorded :— First, of Marjorie Frear, scarcely a year old, in California, which notice was not received in time for last year's record. The infant daughter of Mr. and Mrs. Wm. H. Rice, Jr., born in June after our record was finished, died in less than a month, early in June, 1898. September 26 a son was born to Mr. and Mrs. Wm. H. Shipman, at their Mountain View home, Olaa. This, the tenth child of the family, was a fine, sturdy littl fellow and soon became the idol of the household After the vacation the family returned to Hilo, wher December 12 the life of the darling came to a speed close by accidental scalding, and he went to joi two little brothers gone before. But his *life missio* had been accomplished. Before his death, as the sea of baptism was put on his brow, George Herbert Ship man was enclosed in the same rite with *five other* of the family, thus drawing Jesus very near to their home.

Mrs. Anna (Armstrong) Forbes, wife of Lieut. The

odore F. Forbes, of the U. S. Army, died at Fort Mac-
Pherson, Georgia, Jan. 24, 1899.

Rev. Chas. G. McCully, of Calais, Maine, writes
under date of May 25th : "With deepest grief I am
compelled to say that the name of my beloved daughter, Mary Porter McCully, requires to have the *
affixed to her name as having passed from this world.
She was removed after a few days' illness from ap-
pendicitis, on March 15th last. Her end was peace."

At the breaking of day, June 1st, 1899, Dr. Hugo
Stangenwald finished his life record, and walked among
the angels. It was just 34 years the day he was dying
since Mary Catherine (Dimond) Stangenwald, his first
wife, left him, and their three little ones had also pre-
ceded him. What a joyful reunion ! For many years
Dr. Stangenwald was the trusted and beloved physi-
cian of nearly all the households in Honolulu. His
funeral was largely attended. Our sympathies are
given to the lonely one, Mrs. Annie M. Stangenwald,
who survives him.

Just as this Report was going to press, word was
received of the sudden death, very early in May, of
Miss Lucretia F. Ingraham, of Hunter, N. N. Miss
Ingraham arrived in Hawaii in June, 1873, and was
for three years a most valued assistant in the Kawaiahao Seminary ; then she accepted the position of Principal of the Government Union School in Hilo, where
she was a successful teacher for three years. Re-
signing in 1879, she returned to her home, and has
been an able worker in all church and missionary op-
erations, always retaining her deep aloha for the Hawaiian Islands, and constantly remembering us with
letters. An attack of grippe left her in a very preca-
rious state as to her heart, and death came as she
expected, quite suddenly. A niece, Miss Helen T.
Ingraham, wrote the news of her death, as she had
been requested to.

KAIULANI.

It is impossible to close this year's record of events without a word in memory of the young Princes Kaiulani, who died March 6th, 1899. No more sincere mourners can be four.d than the children of the American Protestant Mission to these islands. We are Hawaiians as well as Americans, and our tears drop now as they did on the day of the Flag Raising, over *"what might have been."* This expression of personal grief was penned in Hilo, when the news first arrived :

I.

Kaiulani! Dear l Beloved!
  Art thou truly fled,
From the nest where thou wast doved ?
  Did I hear it ? Dead ?

Fateful message—do not speed !
  Dead ! Oh, speak it not !
No ! we cannot bear our need !
  See our tears drop hot !

Happy, gentle, full of grace--
  Life so buoyant, bright ;
No ! we cannot yield thy face
  To the fateful night !

II.

Peace, my soul ! Be still, be still,
  'Neath the Heavenly Will !
She of all her Royal race
  Fills undying place.

Love, abiding, still hers below—
  Youth, like spotless snow ;
Life eternal now her boon—
  Heaven came not too soon !

Living now beyond the stars,
  Child of Heaven's King !
Now for thee no sorrow mars
  All the ages bring !

Respectfully submitted.

M. A CHAMBERLAIN,
Corresponding Secretary.

Honolulu, June 3d, 1899.

Educational Report.

Kawaiahao Seminary. Miss Christina W. Paulding, Principal ; Miss Martha A. Myrick, Matron ; Miss Josephine J. Haman, Music Teacher ; Miss Jane E. Johnson, Dressmaking Department ; Miss Belle Johnson, Miss Jessie R. Brockie, Miss Ella Pugsley, Miss Abigail Aikue, Class Room Teachers.

We have had enrolled this year 116 girls. The largest number belonging at one time was ninety six. Of these forty-eight are natives, ten Chinese, four Japanese, one Norwegian, one Portuguese, and the remainder part native. Twenty-eight have been paid for by parents or guardians, and for twenty-two one-half the tuition has been paid in the same way. This is a larger proportion paid for in this way than ever before.

We have had fifteen girls in the dsessmaking department, six of them for but one term. There has been a greater demand for sewing girls than in previous years. The best sewers have been out almost all of the time, leaving only inexperienced girls to do the work taken in. While this has been good for the girls, and is what we are training them for, we have not, in consequence thereof, been able to make as much headway in the department as heretofore. These girls have earned for themselves nearly $700. Five of them paid half their own tuition and one girl paid all of hers. A number of girls have done general house work in families.

The Lima Kokua Society has held its usual monthly meetings. The collections this year were appropriated to the Hawaiian Board, the Woman's Board, the Free Kindergartens, Miss Hoppin's School on Kusaie, the Leper Settlement, a school for blind children in China.

Some of our girls have taught in the Mission Sunday Schools of Pauoa, Kakaako and Maunakiki. Two

have helped regularly in the sewing classes at Palama
Chapel.

The health of the school has been good. We had
measles in the fall and grippe in the spring, but no
serious cases of either disease.

There has been a decided improvement in our girls
this year—an increased spirit of kindness and helpfulness and a greater desire to do their work well, both
in the class rooms and about the house.

We are glad of this opportunity to thank our friends
and patrons who have aided us financially.

CHRISTINA W. PAULDING.

Maunaolu Seminary. As you know, we are in Mrs. Charles H.
Alexander's home and our sixty girls
occupy the old Haleakala school building—that is, they sleep there and we all
eat there, and have our school work and domestic work
in that building. Two of our teachers have rooms
and take charge of girls at night there, while other
teachers sleep in the house of Mrs. Alexander. We
really do remarkably well as regards the comfort of
our large family crowded into such close quarters.

How can we thank the dear Cousins' Society for
remembering our needs so generously? This year, of
all times, is when we need extra funds, and the $300
received recently through your Treasurer was more
appreciated than you will ever quite realize. The
girls whose tuition this will pay are promising and
worthy of trust, we believe. Five of them are daughters of ministers and the sixth one is a real missionary
among her people when at home and has good influence in our school. The ministers to whom the five
belong are Rev. Hanuna of Hana, Maui, Rev. Kalino
of Paia, Maui, and Rev. Nawahine of Waihee, Maui.

Since the old Maunaolu home, so dear to many, was
burned, our girls have had many opportunities to de-

velop graces of character which would never have come to them in the regular routine of school life, and many have surprised us by marked improvement in adaptability, patience, gentleness and real striving to live the Golden Rule.

We are looking forward to our new building for next year.

MARY E. ALEXANDER.

Kohala Girls' School. Our school opened September 5th, and work seems to have commenced at just the point where it was dropped last term. Our faculty was the same as that of last year, until May, when we were glad to add Mrs. Deemer to our number. Mrs. Deemer has charge of the dressmaking department. This is a new department for us, and one of which we felt very much in need. Our girls have always been taught sewing, and a few have gone out sewing by the day; but as we were not able to give them instruction in cutting and fitting, they were in no wise independent in their work. Now, however, they can have that instruction, which will make them independent workwomen and help them to earn a livelihood. Our girls are all very anxious to learn anything which will help them to earn money. Some have earned money this year by going out to do cooking, waiting on table, sewing and teaching native fancy work. One of our girls teaches native work at Ainakea School two days in the week. We are hoping that all the government schools in this district will be allowed teachers in this work next year, for we have girls anxious and competent to teach the same.

Our many kind friends who have helped us in years past have helped us again most generously this year, and not the least of these is the H. M. C. S. The $200 which they have again so generously given our school has been appropriated as follows: Julia Kaihemua, $25 ; Liwai Beright, $25 ; Dorcas Fern, $40 ; Margaret Kaanaana, $25 ; Hannah Molale, $25 ; Ella Kekuewa, $5 ; Minnie Kekuewa, $10 ; Lucy Kapa, $45.

Mr. C. M. Cooke and Mr. H. Waterhouse have aided us very substantially this year. Central Union Sunday School still continues to give the usual $100 for scholarships, and the Kohala Kings Daughters are helpful as ever. This year they have not only given the scholarships, but also a new sewing machine, which is a great help in our dressmaking department.

Our circulars which we have been sending out these last few months, for the purpose of raising an Endowment Fund of $50,000, have been received very pleasantly, and we have had many letters in answer and many promises of help, so we feel much encouraged. This fund, when realized, will place our school upon a firm financial basis, and enable us to increase our appliances and so increase our general usefulness.

Our Christian Endeavor Society is still carrying on its good work, and has proved itself useful and helpful in many ways. The Helping Hand Committee has indeed been appropriately named, and its members proved themselves very efficient during our siege with measles.

Altogether we have had a growing, helpful year, and we are glad of this opportunity to thank so many for sympathy and helpfulness.

MAY BELL TRUETT.

Hilo Boarding School. Our teaching force, with one exception, remains the same as it was last year. In April, Miss Nape found it necessary to resign on account of ill health. Mr. Charles Ellis has acted as substitute in the Primary, while Mrs. J. T. Lewis has come in twice each week to conduct the music classes.

The total number enrolled this year is sixty-five.

While Hilo has passed through a siege of measles, grippe and fever, our boys have been singularly fortunate. We entirely escaped the fever, and the very few cases of measles and grippe were not serious and the victims were soon in their classes again.

Our classes present a cosmopolitan air. At present we enroll, besides the Hawaiians, eight Japanese, two Chinese, four Portuguese and two Germans. While the grown up Japanese men entering the primary class do complicate the work in the primary, we find the presence of other nationalities in the school is beneficial. A wholesome rivalry has been thus introduced.

The time seemed ripe to introduce the subject of starting a Christian Endeavor Society, and in January our Society was organized with fourteen charter members. The Society has grown quietly, the interest has kept up, and good fruits have shown in the lives of the boys.

The boys need no longer break their backs performing their ablutions in the stream. A new lavatory just outside the dormitory acts as a welcome substitute. A coffee-drying house was built last summer vacation in which the school coffee, as well as that for outside parties, has been dried. A few months ago iron piping and other fittings for iron beds were ordered from San Francisco, since which time the boys in the blacksmith department have been busily engaged making beds for their dormitories.

We are indebted to Mrs. Lewis for the kind thought which placed a new piano in our assembly hall. A new dictionary and globe came as a pleasant reminder from a few of the former teachers of the Hilo Boarding School. Plans are now in the hands of carpenters for a new cottage for the lady teachers. With Mr. C. M. Cooke's liberal donation, we believe it will be possible not only to erect this cottage, but also put a coat of paint on all the buildings. With the new cottage and the new paint, two serious needs are supplied. We just as seriously need an extra teacher. The dining hall cannot be looked after as it should be, nor can the little boys—and we have so many little boys—be cared for as they should be with our present small number of teachers. As the means have come here- tofore for other needs as great, we are confident some kind donation will again come to our relief.

We are glad to take this opportunity to thank the Hawaiian Mission Society and others who have so kindly assisted us.

Since writing the above Report, we have been sad- dened by the death of one of our ex–pupils, who died from fever during the epidemic of that disease. He was without a home, so we took him in, but as he failed to improve, we arranged for him to go to the hospital, where he died shortly after.

LEVI C. LYMAN, Principal.

Chinese Mission The "Mills Institute" has continued its important work during the year with a full attendance. Seventy–nine students have been connected with the boarding department, while over fifty day pupils have been con- nected with the institution for a longer or shorter pe- riod. In the school the advance has been steady and satisfactory. A number of our students have taken their stand on the side of Christ and we trust will become leaders and helpers to their people. The young men of our theological training class have been diligent in their studies and assisted most faithfully in various departments of religious and evangelistic work as their time has permitted. We are expecting a strong reinforcement to our teaching force in the near future, two of the three new teachers being graduates this year of Union Theological Seminary of New York City. The kind and generous help afforded us by dif- ferent members of the Cousins' Society, is enabling us to carry forward this educational work which is increasingly proving one of the most important factors in the development of the Chinese Mission.

Our earnest co–worker on Maui, Miss Charlotte Turner, is now absent in the home land, enjoying a period of well earned rest. During her absence Miss Clara Zeigler has most faithfully carried forward her work in the Wailuku School.

Rev. Mr. Lewis writes under recent date, "My impression of the Chinese work on this island is most favorable. It has in it the promise of large results in the near future. I only wish that it might be possible to place more workers in the field."

There is an especially interesting work opening ud in the district of Kula, on the slopes of Haleahala. In Hilo, our little Mission Kindergarten has continued to exert its helpful influence. We have been favored this year in having as principal of our Mahapala (Kohala) School Miss Gertrude Whiteman, who was for a number of years a missionary teacher in Utah. She has taken hold of the work with an earnest spirit and marked ability. Eight of our Chinese girls are enjoying the privileges of the Kohala Seminary. We would like also to refer to the progress of the Chinese girls in Kawaiahao Seminary.

It is a great pleasure and satisfaction to have associated with us in our missionary work one who is directly in the line of "cousinly" descent. Since the beginning of this year Miss Mable Sunter has been working among the Chinese women and girls of the city and suburbs, under appointment from the Woman's Board. She has entered energetically and enthusiastically upon her work, and found her way into many homes, where she has been warmly welcomed. She has begun the study of the Chinese language, in which she is making good progress. She states that already she has come into contact with nearly six hundred women, and that many more are yet to be visited. Most truly does she say, "On every side are

open doors of opportunity bidding one enter. The
work is a blessed one, but to it must be brought the
zeal and wisdom of the Master, without whom we can
do nothing." God grant that others from the ranks
of our young cousins may be led to give themselves to
active missionary work.

Respectfully submitted,

FRANK W. DAMON.

Treasurer's Report.

RECEIPTS.

Balance from last year's account......................$ 70 30
Ten collections, including pledges.................... 121 60
From Bond fund....................................... 269 75
Sale of Micronesian curios........................... 37 35
Donations from abroad :

Miss Blair ....$	1 00	
Miss Laura C. Green	3 00	
Sara L. King.....................	3 00	
Helen E. Carpenter.....	10 00	
Chas. A. Colcord	20 00	
		37 00

Donations from the Islands :

Maria R. Forbes ....$	1 00	
Wm. J. Forbes	5 00	
W. D. Alexander	10 00	
Helen S. Judd....	10 00	
Mrs. Maria J. Forbes............ ..	20 00	
F. J. Lowrey...........◡.............	25 00	
W. F. Frear	25 00	
W. R. Castle.................	60 00	
S. M. Damon	230 00	
Geo. P. Castle	250 00	
A. S. Wilcox..................	250 00	
H. P. Baldwin....................	500 00	
Mr. and Mrs. C. M. Cooke	1000 00	
		2386 00

Twenty-eight Life Membership fees:
 Frederick Chambers Baldwin,
 Charlotte McKinney Baldwin
 Samuel Alexander Baldwin
 Horace Emery Coleman,
 Mrs. Floy Rhode Coleman,
 Joseph Platt Cooke,
 Emily Montague Cooke,
 Mrs. Lily Love Cooke,
 Henry Fowler Damon,
 Douglas Wilfrid Damon,
 Mrs. Clara Kennedy De La Vergne,
 Mary Ferreira,
 Mrs. Frances A. Stevens Gulick,
 Bessie Templeton Hopper,
 Mrs. Margaret Hare Howard,
 Kate Kelley,
 Frances E. Lawrence,
 Emily B. Montague,
 Christina Wood Paulding,
 Silas P. Perry,
 Mrs. Ellida Olsson Perry,
 Philip Adam de la Porte,
 Mrs. Salome de la Porte,
 Mary Agnes Rice,
 Evelyn Henrietta Schoen,
 Anna Kathrine Smith,
 Lorrin Knapp Smith,
 Mrs. Isabel Ferreira Tarbell,   280 00

Ten Annual Membership fees:
 Lorrin Andrews,
 Horace E. Coleman,
 Mrs. Floy R. Coleman,
 C. W. Dickey,
 Mrs. Selma S. Kinney,
 Henry Walsworth Kinney,
 Maud Miriam Kinney,
 Rev. A. V. Soares,
 Mrs. A. V. Soares,
 Philip L. Weaver,   10 00

  Total receipts........................$3212 40

EXPENDITURES.

APPROPRIATIONS OF LAST YEAR UNPAID AT LAST ACCOUNT.

Aid to Schools of Chinese Mission..........$ 12 00
Support of Pupils in Hilo Boys' Boarding School 50 00
"   "   E. Maui Female Seminary, 100 00
Aid to Portuguese Mission Work............ 100 00
Aid to Japanese Mission Work 100 00
Salaries of Corresponding Secretaries 100 00

Total of last year's appropriations paid $ 562 00

THIS YEAR'S APPROPRIATIONS.

Support of Teachers in Kawaiahao Seminary $150 00
"   " Pupils   "   "   "   200 00
"   "   "   " E. Maui Female Sem'y 200 00
"   "   "   " Kohala Girls' School 200 00
"   "   "   " Hilo Boys' Boarding
                                         School.......... 200 00
Aid of Schools of Chinese Mission 200 00
"   Portuguese Mission Work........... 200 00
"   Japanese Mission Work 100 00
"   Mortlock Teachers and Evangelists... 300 00
"   Missionary on Pleasant Island........ 100 0C
Salary of Corresponding Secretaries......... 100 00
Publishing Annual Report 97 00
Fxpense of Mailing Annual Report 8 00
Printing Circulars 2 50
Printing Life Membership Certificates...... 3 50

2061 00
Total expenditures................. .... 2623 00

Balance on hand June 1, 1899............... 589 00

This balance will be a surprise to those who read the Treasurer's appeal a little over a month ago, showing a shortage of $2,000. It shows with what heartiness the Cousins rally to the support of their Society when they know its need.

LEA. DICKEY, Treasurer.

Address of the Retiring President, Rev. J. Leadingham.

The Industrial Education Needed in Hawaii and the Incentives to It.

" The shoemaker should stick to his last," is an old adage which everyone who ventures into a discussion on a subject outside of his own sphere would do well to remember. Still, what we ourselves do in one direction may be so modified by what some one else does or fails to do in another direction, that for the proper guidance of our own work we are forced at times to formulate opinions on subjects in regard to which our experience is limited. This is my excuse for attempting to write on the topic I have named. For the sake of brevity and clearness, I will introduce the suggestions which I have to make by relating in outline the story of an industrial experiment which for the past ten years has been carried on in another place— that of the Industrial Missionary Association of Alabama.

In 1878, Rev. C. B. Curtis and wife, then under the American Missionary Association, went to Selma, Alabama, and began labor with the colored Congregational Church in that city. " There, in direct personal contact with the people, they studied the needs of the then recently emancipated freedmen. The conclusion was forced upon them that, while existing missionary activities should be continued, there was a demand for work upon a new plan, especially in back ward sections remote from missionary centres. Nine-tenths of the colored population then lived on plantations, most of them beyond the reach of intelligent preaching and good schools. There vice and ignorance seemed on the increase, and the people's condition was appalling."

The plan of Mr. and Mrs. Curtis was to supplement religious instruction and mental training by giving

the people the opportunity to secure homes for them
selves, and, in the meantime, to train them in habits of
thrift and correct methods of work. This involved
the purchase of a tract of land, which was to be rented
or sold to the people in smaller tracts. All the labor
connected with the cultivation and management of
this land was, of course, to be under the direction of
competent oversight. Alongside of this manual part
of the work, the church life was to be kept up and
the public school system maintained, supplemented,
as occasion required, by aid from rents and other
revenues of the business. By this method, it was
intended that families which took up the land of the
Association should eventually become independent
owners of farms, while the family life would be safe-
guarded and a purer and more intelligent social condition developed. It was a part of the theory also
that the enterprise should be in great part self-
supporting.

The attempt was made to induce the older missionary organizations to take up the work, but they were
incorporated for educational and religious purposes
and could not go into the business of buying and
selling land. Mr. and Mrs. Curtis were, therefore,
obliged either to give up their effort, or to sever their
connection with the Missionary Association under
which they had labored and form a new Society.
They chose the latter course, and, to test their scheme,
bought 300 acres of land, and began renting as pro-
posed. The results were encouraging, and Mr. Curtis,
with some other gentlemen co-operating with him,
secured a certificate of incorporation and thus placed
the new society on a legal basis.

This was in 1888. Much sacrifice and labor were
necessary in securing funds and beginning the work,
but the beginning was made, and the enterprise pros
pered. A brief extract from a report written in the
year 1897 will show the progress made in the first

eight years. This report speaks as follows of the work :

" It is successful. Incorporated in 1888, its first year's work in 1889 began with 400 acres and a few families, and its last year, 1896, reported 4000 acres, between 60 and 70 families, 1 school in 3 departments, 3 other schools, really 6 day schools in all, 2 night schools, 4 Sunday schools maintained or aided, 2 churches, a farmers' club, cotton gin and press, saw mill and grist mill for corn, store, post office, freight office, and an actual business profit of $3647.51. This last feature, business profit, has made decided progress. The year 1892, the first with the present area, incurred a loss on account of short crops and low prices, together with the inevitable difficulties of a new enterprise ; 1893 showed a small profit ; 1894 a profit of $1455.16 ; 1895, $2173.96 ; and 1896, $3674.51. Already the business receipts are more than sustaining the local mission. From extreme poverty, negro families have advanced in equipment for home and farm, and are feeling the thrill of opportunity and a better life."

Now, do we find any suggestion from this brief story for the solution of industrial problems here ? We have here a large class of young men and women of different nationalities growing up who have no present connection with any kind of industrial life that is of common interest to the whole family, as is the case with a farmer's children in the older agricultural communities. The father is usually a common laborer. The children have no responsibility for a home establishment, and so are always in danger of getting into mischief. The larger part of them go to school, it is true, but, aside from their mental training, gain but little which fits them to take places in the industrial life of the land. It is to be remembered also that these children are poor. They have not the means when they reach young manhood and womanhood of establishing themselves in independent lines of work. They could

do this, if at all, only after long years of steady service and careful economy, at low wages. Under
these conditions but very few would ever outgrow the
condition of the common day laborer.

On the other hand, there is still in these islands a
large amount of undeveloped land suited to division
into small tracts and capable of supporting a varied
industry. Our agricultural resources have not yet
begun to be developed either in extent or variety.
Hilo grass, bushes and other kinds of vegetation,
cover our mountain sides from bottom to the top.
Why cannot these wild products of nature be replaced
by some form of growth that would be productive to
the planter and afford a healthful and independent
employment for himself and family?

We have here, then, a large quantity of undeveloped
brain and muscle, and a large amount of undeveloped
land suited to agricultural uses. Is it not true that
one of the great problems facing the people of the
Islands to-day is to bring these two classes of undeveloped resources together for their mutual improvement ? Is it not simple justice that the poorest
classes, so far as they are worthy, should have the
opportunity of obtaining such property rights as will
make their lot in life easier, and inspire in them a
desire for higher character and usefulness ? Does not
the future stability and safety of the country require
this? It is a very trite observation that the strength
of a country lies in its agricultural class. The same
should be true here. If there cannot be a strong
agricultural class created, the country will always lack
that element which furnishes backbone and stability
to the social fabric. If the land in large tracts passes
into the hands of corporations or wealthy individuals,
the poor cannot easily get it, and the population must
always remain what it is now—a few people of large
wealth, a very large and very poor laboring class,
and between these a small class in moderate and com-
fortable circumstances. Such a state of affairs is un-

favorable to the growth of the highest type of character. It smothers ambition in the poorer class by rendering them unable to secure the conditions which are necessary to their advancement. It consequently makes the support of all benevolent and philanthropic work dependent upon the gifts of the wealthy. Under this system the population may be analysed according to another principle of division. We have not simply a very wealthy class and a very poor class, but a class which becomes the dispenser of charity, and another which, for everything above the elements of a meagre existence, depends on charity. This class comes in time to lose its self–respect and energy in caring for itself, and to look more and more to the charity-dispensing class to provide for it.

I will illustrate what I mean by a single example. In the North Pacific Missionary Institute we are trying to raise up a class of young men who shall serve the different races of the Islands as pastors. Most of these men have been in the higher schools, when they have had new desires awakened and become accustomed to a more elevated style of living than they formerly found in the homes of their parents. Moreover, go almost where they will to-day and they find themselves surrounded by foreigners, who main-tain this higher and better kind of living. Their work throws them more and more into contact with this class of people. They are, therefore, compelled, both by the new impulses which they feel in themselves and by the necessities of their surroundings, to attempt a better style of living than was customary a few years ago.

Now, when these men go out to work among the churches what do they find? The churches will gene-rally promise to pay them some specified sum, but, unless stimulated and aided by some outside influence, such as a pastor's aid society, they will almost in–variably fail to keep their faith. I am speaking now of the Hawaiian churches. These are becoming poorer and more dependent on the support of foreigners.

The situation is full of danger to the pastor as well as to the church. His salary is too small at best, and under the conditions I have described he is almost certain to become involved in obligations that he cannot meet, not necessarily because he has any inclination to do so, but from the nature of the circumstances. When he once becomes thus involved it is almost impossible for him to get out of the difficulty, and he is driven either to make appeals to men of wealth, and thus to receive the aid of charity, or to a life of makeshifts which brings him under the censure of those who know him, and subjects him to the damaging effects on character which always accompany a failure to meet one's obligations.

Now what is needed to save both churches and pastors is the creation among the people of some productive industry, and about the only one which can be relied upon for the greater part of the people is that connected with the cultivation of land.

With the other races the case is not essentially different. If they are to become capable of maintaining the institutions which will elevate them, they must in some way form a background of independent, self-sustaining industries. If they do not, then, for them too, every thing above the bare necessities of life must be furnished by the charity of the wealthy class, and the grounds of self-respect and ambition taken from them.

It will become evident at this point why one who is engaged in the work of theological education should turn his mind to the industrial problem. It is because he sees the intimate relation between the moral and material conditions of the people, and that the success of the one depends on the prosperity of the other.

Again we ask, then, do we find any helpful suggestion from the history of the industrial missionary of Alabama? I believe we do. We have lately seen a growing interest here in furnishing instruction in agricultural subjects, and something is now being done along this line in the government schools. But we may fairly raise the question whether this goes far enough. What incentive is there at present for the great majority of children to study in this direction? A boy who has no land, and who has no reasonable expectation that he can raise money to purchase it with the necessary outfit, and meet the expense of clearing and planting, probably will not become greatly interested in the effort. Besides, it would hardly seem possible in connection with the public school system to teach more than a few of the simplest and easiest processes and facts connected with the subject. But suppose the Government or some public spirited man of wealth should appropriate a tract of land for this purpose, and invite young men, under competent direction, to do the work of clearing, fencing, tilling, planting, and caring for crops till they were ready for market, with the understanding that, when they had become proficient in the work, and the land had been brought under cultivation, they would be rewarded for their service by having the opportunity to rent or purchase a portion of the same on such favorable terms that they might reasonably expect in a short time to have a home and farm of their own, would there not be in this an incentive strong enough to induce many a young man to make the effort?

I have not forgotten the shoemaker and his last, but it seems that such a plan is feasable, and that many advantages would attend it. The men who might acquire property in this way would be, in a degree at least, trained agriculturists before the experiment of being independent farmers was tried. There would hence be less danger of ultimate failure. What any one might gain, would be gained by his own effort and would be a training in self respect and manliness. The method should become a self–sustaining and progressive one. Let the returns from the first one or two crops accrue to the managing body. This, with the subsequent revenues from rents and sales, would help meet the expense of acquiring and reducing more land.

Here, too, the expense would be less than that involved in the work of the Industrial Association of Alabama, as it would be confined mostly to the actual development of the land. In the matter of schools and churches, there would not need to be so much outlay, as we could make use of the churches and church work already established; and if the work was for young men mostly, instead of families, there would be less call for expense in education. In any case, the government school system would probably meet most of the need.

I am well aware that there would be difficulties connected with such an enterprise which cannot be explained away on paper. To be of service and to be successful it would not be a temporary experiment, but an institution running parallel with the other educational and industrial institutions of the land, and designed to elevate the people and to cultivate in them an enlightened interest in the welfare and stability of the country. It is certainly the duty of every one to study our present situation and to ask himself, what we are coming to? We do not wish to become an anomaly in the sisterhood of States and Territories to which we now politically belong, but rather by the cultivation of morality, intelligence, and healthful and productive industry, to be worthy of a place in the esteem of America and the world.

Constitution and By-Laws.

We, the children of the American Protestant Mission to the Hawaiian Islands, desiring to promote the cause of Gospel Missions, as well as to strengthen the bond of union that naturally exists among us, do hereby organize ourselves into a Social Missionary Society, under the following Constitution and By-Laws:

CONSTITUTION.

ARTICLE I. This Society shall be called "THE HAWAIIAN MISSION CHILDREN'S SOCIETY."

ART. 2. The design of the Society is to cherish and promote union among its members, to cultivate in them an active missionary spirit, stir them up to good work, and more especially to assist in the support of Christian Missions.

ART. 3. The officers of the Society shall be a President, Vice-President, Recording Secretary, two or more Corresponding Secretaries, and a Treasurer, all of whom shall be elected by ballot at the annual meeting of the Society, to hold office for one year.

ART. 4. No one is eligible to fill the office of President for two consecutive years.

ART. 5. At each annual meeting of the Society, two members shall be chosen by ballot, who, together with the officers mentioned in Article 3, and such members as may be chosen by the Auxiliary Societies in accordance with Article 9, shall constitute a Board of Managers, and who shall hold office for one year.

Art. 6. Any descendant of those who are or have been members of the American Protestant Mission to these islands, and the descendants of all those admitted into the Society in accordance with Article 7, are entitled to join the Society by paying into the Treasury the sum of one dollar annually, which shall constitute one an annual member, or paying at any one time the sum of ten dollars, which shall constitute one a Life Member.

ART. 7. Any other persons in active sympathy with the objects and aims of the Society, may become members by recommendation of the Board of Managers, approved by a two-thirds vote of the members present at any regular meeting of the Society, on payment of fees as in Article 6.

ART. 8. Any number of Life Members, resident elsewhere than in Honolulu, pledging not less than $20 annually to the Treasurer of this Society, may form an "Auxiliary" (to consist of Annual and Life Members of the Society) by the appointment of such officers, and the making of such regulations as they may wish ; provided, however, all be done in conformity with Article 2 of the Constitution.

ART.9. Any Auxiliary Society pledging not less than $100 per annum shall be entitled to elect annually one member of the Board of Managers of the Parent Society, to hold office one year from its annual meeting.

ART. 10. All members of the American Protestant Mission are *ex officio* Honorary Members of this Society. Any person may be admitted as an Honorary Member of this Society by the consent of a majority of the Board of Managers, approved by a two-thirds vote of the members present at any regular meeting of the Society.

ART. 11. Any member may appeal from any action of the Board of Managers. If the appeal is seconded, such action may be reversed by a majority vote of the members present.

ART. 12. The Society shall hold a regular meeting on such a Saturday evening of each month as it may approve, or at the call of the President, and an annual meeting in May or June.

ART. 13. Each member shall receive a certificate of membership in the following form, to be signed by the

President and countersigned by the Treasurer.

<table>
<tr><td>Charity suffereth long and is kind ; not easily provoked, and thinketh no evil.—Cor. xiii:4-5.</td><td>

Behold how good and how pleasant it is for brothers to dwell together in unity.—Ps. cxxiii:1.

𝔗𝔥𝔦𝔰 𝔐𝔞𝔶 ℭ𝔢𝔯𝔱𝔦𝔣𝔶 𝔱𝔥𝔞𝔱

- -

Having paid the sum of..... *Dollars into the Treasury, is a*.................*Member of the*

Hawaiian Mission Children's Society.

Honolulu............*18*..

(*Signed*) ....
                                    President.

....
              Treasurer.

Go ye into all the world and preach the Gospel to every creature.—Mark xvi:15.

</td><td>One generation passeth away and another cometh, but the earth abideth forever.—Eccl. i:4.</td></tr>
</table>

ART. 14. Alterations in, or additions to, this Constitution may be made at any regular meeting by a vote of three fourths of the members present, such alterations or additions having been handed in, in writing, at the previous meeting through the Board of Managers.

BY-LAWS.

ARTICLE I.—OF THE OFFICERS.

SECTION 1. The President shall preside over the meetings of the Society, deliver an address before the Society at its annual meeting, upon vacating his office; appoint all committees not otherwise provided for; sign all certificates of membership, arrange the programme of exercises for each regular meeting, consulting with the chairmen of the various committees, and he may convene the Society to special meetings at his discretion. He shall also be *ex-officio* President of the Board of Managers.

SEC. 2. The Vice-President shall audit the annual Report of the Treasurer, and perform all the duties of the President in case of his absence.

SEC. 3. It shall be the duty of the Recording Secretary to keep a record of the proceedings of the Society at its several meetings, and make out an abstract report of the proceedings of the Society, during his term of office, at its annual meeting. He shall also be *ex-officio* Secretary of the Board of Managers, and shall furnish the Treasurer with a certified copy of every order on the Treasurer authorized by the Board.

SEC. 4. The Corresponding Secretaries shall carry on the correspondence of the Society at home and abroad; take charge of the books and papers of the Society, excepting the files of the *Maile Wreath*, and report at its annual meeting.

SEC 5. The Treasurer shall receive and safely keep all moneys belonging to the Society, pay over such moneys as may be directed from time to time by the Board of Managers, for the purpose of defraying such expenses as shall have been incurred by their order, such order having the signature of the Recording Secretary; shall countersign all certificates of membership; and shall, at the annual meeting of the Society, present an accurate statement of the receipts and disbursements of the Society during the year.

ARTICLE II.—OF THE BOARD OF MANAGERS.

SEC. 1. It shall be the duty of the Board of Managers to superintend all business transactions of the Society not otherwise provided for in the Constitution, and to keep full and correct minutes of all its own proceedings

SEC. 2. Any member of the Society desiring to bring any business before the Board of Managers, shall make known such business in a written application to some member of the Board, who shall lay it before the Board for their action thereon.

SEC. 3. The Board shall decide upon all applications for membership under Articles 7 and 10 of the Constitution; and also upon the disposition of the funds of the Society.

SEC. 4. The minutes of the Board shall be read before the Society at each regular meeting for acceptance and adoption.

SEC. 5. Any vacancies occurring in the Board of Managers, by death or otherwise, shall be refilled by regular election of the Society at the earliest succeeding meeting.

SEC. 6. The regular meetings of the Board shall be held at such times as the Board may determine, within seven days immediately preceding the regular meeting of the Society. The Secretary of the Board shall note the members present at each meeting.

SEC. 7. Special meetings of the Board may be called by the President at his discretion, or by three members thereof.

ARTICLE III.—DUTIES OF MEMBERS.

The members of the Society are expected to attend the regular meetings of the Society, as far as may be possible; to perform all such duties as may from time to time be assigned to them; to collect all information that may be useful or interesting to the Society, and at each regular meeting to contribute to the funds of the Society, according to their generosity and means.

ARTICLE IV.—OF MEETINGS.

The regular monthly meetings of the Society shal be opened by prayer and singing; the minutes of the last meeting shall be read by the Recording Secretary; the minutes of the Board of Managers shall then be read and acted upon; a collection shall be taken up by the Treasurer; the entertainment provided for in Article 5 shall then be in order; next shall follow miscellaneous business; after which the meeting shall be closed by singing.

The monthly meetings of the Society shall be open to such guests as any of the members may invite as being in sympathy with the Society and its objects.

ARTICLE V.—STANDING COMMITTEE.

There shall be a committee of one on music, who shall be chosen quarterly, to aid in providing for the profitable entertainment of each monthly meeting.*

There shall be a committee of four, consisting of two ladies and two gentlemen, to be elected every four months, to conduct a monthly paper, the purpose of which shall be to develop more fully the intellectual resources of the Society, and add to the missionary interest of each monthly meeting.

There shall be a committee of one, to be appointed annually, whose duty it shall be to provide the editors of the *Maile Wreath* with suitable stationary, and to be responsible for the safe keeping of the file of the *Maile Wreath*.

ARTICLE VI.—RULES OF ORDER.

SEC. 1. In Miscellaneous Business, no one shall speak more than five minutes at a time, without permission from the Society.

SEC. 2. In all points of order, the presiding officer shall be guided by the rules laid down in Cushing's Manual.

ARTICLE VII.

These By-Laws may be altered or annulled by a vote of two—thirds of the members present at any regular meeting, notice of each amendment having been given at the meeting next preceding.

---

* By resolution of the Society, the President, with two elective members of the Board of Managers, shall constitute a committee on entertainment whose duty it shall be to secure additional attractions for our regular meetings, especially in the line of address or lectures.

Names and Place of Residence of Members.

HONORARY MEMBERS.

NOT OF THE HAWAIIAN MISSION.

Miss Annie E. Abell	Buffalo, N Y
Rev. James R. Boyd, D. D.*	
Mrs. James R. Boyd *	
Rev. Irving M. Channon	Kusaie, Caroline Islands
Mrs. Mary G. Channon	" " "
Miss E .Theodora Crosby	New York City, N. Y.
Rev. Edward T. Doane *	
Mrs. Sarah W. Doane *	
Miss Clara S. Doane	Elgin, Ill
Miss Jennie E. Fletcher	Carthage, Ill
Mrs. Rachel C. Forbes	Montreal, Canada
Miss Ida M. Foss	West Woodstock, Conn.
Mrs. Sarah L. (Smith) Garland	"Morning Star"
Rev. Dr. William Goodell *	
Miss Jessie M. Hoppin	Kusaie, Caroline Islands
Rev. Albert S. Houston	Gilman, Iowa
Mrs. Lizzie S. Houston	" "
Rev. Robert G. Hutchins, D. D.	Cleveland, Ohio
Miss Lucy M. Ingersoll, M. D.	Escondido, Cal
Miss Rose Kinney	Oberlin, Ohio
Mrs. T. W. Knight *	
Rev. Rudolph Lechler	Hongkong, China
Mrs. Maria Lechler	" "
Miss Alice Little	Oberlin, Ohio
Rev. Robert W. Logan*	
Mrs. Mary E. Logan	Truk, Mortlock
Mrs. Elizabeth Mead	Mt. Holyoke Col., South Hadley, Mass.
Mrs Lydia (Hemingway) Morehouse	Le Roy, Ill
Miss Jennie Olin,	Kusaie, Caroline Is.
Miss Annette A. Palmer	Cedar Rapids, Iowa
Rev. Edward M. Pease, M. D.	Claremont, Cal
Mrs. Harriet A Pease	"
Rev. Dr. Peck	New York
Rev. George Pierson*	
Mrs. N. Annette Pierson*	
Rev. Francis M. Price	Truk, Mortlock
Mrs. Sarah J. Price	"
Rev. Frank E. Rand	West Woodstock, Conn
Mrs. Carrie E. Rand	" "
Dr. Clinton F Rife	Kusaie, Caroline Islands
Mrs. Isadora Rife	" "
Miss Lydia W. Shattuck*	

*Deceased.

Rev. Alfred Snelling - -	Truk, Mortlock Islands
Mrs. Elizabeth N. Snelling -	" "
Rev. Albert A. Sturgess*	
Mrs. Susan M. Sturgess*	
Rev. B. Galen Snow*	
Mrs. Lydia V. Snow*	
Rev. Arthur H. Smith, D. D. -	Pang Chuang, China
Mrs. Emma D. Smith - -	"
Rev. Horace J. Taylor - -	Kellogsville, Ohio
Mrs. Julia A. Taytor*	
Mrs. Jennie R. Taylor*	
Rev. Daniel J. Treiber - -	Ipswich, South Dakota
Mrs. D. J. Treiber	" "
Rev. Alfred C. Walkup - -	Apaiang, Gilbert Islands
Mrs. Venie M. Walkup*	
Rev. William D. Westervelt -	Honolulu, Oahu
Mrs. Louie C. Westervelt	"
Rev. Joel F. Whitney - -	Eldred, N Y
Mrs. Louisa M. Whitney	"
Miss Louise Wilson - -	Kusaie, Caroline Islands

LIFE MEMBERS.

All the absent members of this Society are hereby requested to assist in correcting this list of names, as many errors have undoubtedly crept in.

Any changes in name by marriage, or any errors in the place of residence, are particularly desired.

Photographs of absent members may be sent to either of the Corresponding Secretaries.

Adams, Anna H.† - - -	Boston, Mass
Adams, Rev. John Q. - - -	Clifton Springs, N Y
" Mrs. Clara S. - - -	" "
Aea, Hezekiah - - - -	Honolulu, Oahu
" Rachel*	
Aiken, Mrs. Jennie (Willis) - -	Fall River, Mass
Aiken, Worth O. - - -	Hamakuapoko, Maui
" Mrs. Helen M. (Chamberlain)	" "
Ailau, Mrs. Mary (Pitman) - -	Honolulu, Oahu
Alexander, William De Witt -	" "
" Mrs. Abigail (Baldwin)	" "

*Deceased. † Member of Ladies' Society of Essex Street Church, Boston.

"	Wm. Douglas - -	"
"	Henry E. Mansfield -	California
"	Mary Charlotte - -	Traveling in Europe
"	Agnes Baldwin -	Honolulu, Oahu
Alexander,	Arthur Chambers -	Berkeley, Cal
"	Mrs. Mary E. (Hillebrand)	" "
"	William Patterson ..	" "
"	Helen Constance ..	
"	Arthur De Witt - ..	" "
Alexander,	Rev. James McKinney	Oakland, Cal
"	Mrs. Mary (Webster)	" "
"	Frank Alvan - -	Hamakuapoko, Maui
"	Mary Edith - -	Oakland, Cal
"	Edgar Wm - -	" "
"	Sarah Eva - - -	" "
Alexander,	Samuel Thomas - -	
"	Mrs. Martha (Cooke) -	..
"	Juliette - - -	"
"	Annie Montgomery -	"
"	Wallace McKinney -	
Alexander,	Mary J. - - -	.. ..
Alexander,	Charles Hodge*	
"	Mrs. Helen (Thurston)	Honolulu, Oahu
"	Charles Frederick -	" "
"	Helen Andrews - -	" "
Alexander,	Henry Martin - -	Anderson, Cal
"	Charlotte Ellen -	Siena, Italy
Alexander,	Mary E., Prin. Maunaolu Seminary, Makawao, Maui.	
Allen,	Col. Wm. Fessenden -	Honolulu, Oahu
"	Mrs. Cordelia (Bishop) -	" "
Andrews,	Lorrin, Jr.	
Andrews,	Robert W. - - -	Honolulu, Oahu
"	Mrs. Rosina S.*	.. "
"	Robert Standard - -	.. ..
"	Carl Bowers - -	" "
"	Mrs. Maria (Sheeley) -	
Andrews,	Samuel - - -	Makua, Oahu
Andrews,	William - - -	Brooklyn. N Y
"	Mrs. Adele (Oscanyan)	" "
Andrews,	Samuel C. - - -	New York City
"	Mabel A. - - -	" "
Andrews,	Lucy C. _p_ - - -	E. Orange, N J
"	Lorrin A. - - -	Hilo, Hawaii
Andrews,	Dr. George P. - .	Honolulu, Oahu
"	Mrs. Sarah (Dyer) -	" "
"	Winifred Parnelly -	Detroit, Michigan

---

* Deceased. _p_ Photograph.

Appleby, Mrs. Grace (Colcord) - Woburn, Mass
   "   Henry Colcord*
   "   Florence A.   -   -   "   "
Appleton, Lilla E.   -   -   -   Damon's Crossing, Vt
Armstrong, William Nevins   -   Honolulu, Oahu
   "   Mrs. Mary F. (Morgan)   Hampton, Vir
   "   Matthew C.   -   -   "   "
   "   Richard Baxter   -   "   "
   "   Morgan Halani   -   Yale Col, New Hav, Conn
   "   Dorothy -   -   -   Hampton, Vir
Armstrong, General Samuel C.*
   "   Mrs. Emma (Walker)*
   "   Louise H.   -   -
       Mrs. Mary Alice   -
   "   Margaret Marshall   -
   "   Daniel Williams   -   "   "
Armstrong, Mary J.   -   -   -   San Francisco, Cal
   "   Amelia   -   -   -   Oakland, Cal
Arundel, John T.   -   -   -   London, Eng
Atherton, Joseph B   -   -   -   Honolulu, Oahu
   "   Mrs. Juliette (Cooke) -   "   "
   "   Benjamin H.*
   "   Alexander M. John Hopkins' Med. Schl., Baltimore, Md
   "   Frank Cooke   -   -   Honolulu, Oahu
   "   Kate Marion   -   -   "   "
Atherton, Caroline*
   "   Charles Henry   -   -
   "   Mrs. Minnie (Merriam)
   "   Violet Merriam   -   -
   "   Juliette Montague   -
   "   Laura Annis   -   -
Atwater, William O.   -   -   -
   "   Mrs. E. (Baldwin)*
   "   Mrs. Annie E. (Benner)   "   "
Atwater, Mrs. Lilian (Baldwin) -   Haiku, Maui
Austin, Stafford L.*
   "   Mrs. Caroline H. (Clark) -   Oakland, Cal
   "   Franklin H.   -   -   -   Honolulu, Oahu
   "   Herbert Clark -   -   -   "   "
   "   Benjamin Hale*
Bailey, Edward Hubbard   -   -   Wailuku, Maui
Bailey, Horatio Bardwell   -   -   Makawao, Maui
Bailey, William Hervey   -   -   Oakland, Cal
   "   Mrs. Annie (Hobron)   -   "   "
   "   Minnie Hobron   -   -   "   "
   "   Wm. Hervey, Jr.   -   -

* Deceased.

Bailey, James Clark*
Bailey, Charles Aldin - - - Anaheim, Cal
" Mrs. Jessie (Cameron) - " "
Balding, Mrs. Caroline (Clark) - Wainaku, Hilo, Hawaii
Baldwin, David Dwight - - Haiku, Maui
" Mrs. Lois (Morris) - " "
" Erdman Dwight - - Hilo, Hawaii
" Charles Wickliffe - - Haiku, Maui
" Lincoln Mansfield - Wailuku, Maui
" Benjamin Douglas - Hamakuapoko, Maui
" William Atwater - - Makaweli, Kauai
" Nathaniel H.*
Baldwin, Charles F.*
Baldwin, Henry Perrine - - Haiku, Maui
" Mrs. Emily (Alexander) " "
" William Dwight - - Baltimare, Md
" Arthur Douglas - - Cambridge, Mass
" Frank Fowler - - Haiku, Maui
" Frederick Chambers - Lakeville, Conn
" Charlotte McKinney - Haiku, Maui
" Samuel Alexander - " · "
Baldwin, Henry Alexander - - Hamakuapoko, Maui
" Mrs. Ethel (Smith) - " "
" Leslie Alexander - - " "
Baldwin, Samuel E.*
Baldwin, Willie Dane - - . West Groton, Mass
Banning, Frederick*
" Mrs. Clara (Armstrong) Oakland, Cal
" Bernardt Rudolph - - " "
" Frederick Armstrong*
" Richard Armstrong*
Barnett, Joseph - - - Kohala, Hawaii
Bartlett, George L. - - - Charleston, Mass
Bates, Dudley C. - - - San Francisco, Cal
Beardsley, Grove, M. D. - - Navy Yd, Charleston, Mass
Beckwith, Rev. Edward Griffin *p* - Paia, Maui
" Mrs. Caroline (Armstrong) *p* " "
Beckwith, Rev. Frank Armstrong*
" Mrs. Ellen (Holmes) Montclair, N J
" Ruth Holmes - - " "
" Frank Holmes - - " "
Beckwith, George Ely*
" Mrs. Harriet (Goodale) Marlboro, Mass
" Mary Goodale - - " "
" George Edward*
" Martha Warren - - Traveling in Europe

*Deceased. *p* Photograph.

Beckwith, Morris Goodale - - Frederick, Md.
Benfield, Marcus*
Benfield, Mrs. Mary (Thurston)*
   "   Erick Lex*
   "   Lily J.*
   "   Ida*
Bicknell, Mrs. Ellen (Bond) - • Honolulu, Oahu
   "   James - - - -   "   "
   "   Ellen H. - - - Kamehameha Preparatory
   "   George - • - - Honolulu, Oahu
   "   William B . - - Worcester, Mass
Bindt, Mrs. Louisa (Johnson)*
   "   Julia Lois*
   "   Bertha Frances - - - Peninsula, Oahu
   "   Paul Rudolph - - - Honolulu, Oahu
   "   Ernest A. - - - - California
Bingham, Rev. Hiram, D. D. - Honolulu, Oahu
   "   Mrs. Clara (Brewster) -   "   "
   "   Hiram, Jr. - - - California
Bingham, Elizabeth K. - • Honolulu, Oahu
Birnie, Rev. Douglas Putnam - Rye, N Y City
Bishop, Rev. Sereno Edwards, D.D. *p* Honolulu, Oahu
   "   Mrs. Cornelia Sessions -   "   "
   "   Edward F.*
Bishop, John Sessions, M. D. - Astoria, Oregon
   "   Mrs. Alice (Moore) - • "   "
   "   Helen Cornelia - - "   "
   "   John Egbert - - - ..   "
Bishop, Bradley*
Bissel, Rev. Edwin C., D. D.*
   "   Mrs. Emily Pomeroy - Somers, Conn
Bliss, Miss Hattie M - - - Pasadena, Cal
Bond, George S. - • - - Kohala, Hawaii
Bond, Elias Cornelius - - - "   "
   "   Robert Elias - - Yale Col., New Haven, Ct
   "   Edith Howell - - West Bridgewater, Mass
Bond, T. Spencer*
   "   William Lee - - - Fairview, Mich
   "   Caroline S. - - - Kohala, Hawaii
   "   Abbie Steele *p* - - - Batavia, Ill
Bond, Julia P, - - - Kohala, Hawaii
Bond, Benjamin D., M. D. - - "   "
   "   Mrs. Emma (Renton) - "   "
   "   Benjamin Howell - -
   "   Alice Renton - - -
   "   Kenneth Davis -

---

* Deceased. *p* Photograph.

Bowen, William A. - - -	Honolulu, Oahu
" Mrs. Emma (Kennedy) -	" "
" William Spencer . -	" "
" Mary Elizabeth Zilla*	
Boyd, Nettie E. - - - -	Calais, Me
Brewer, Prof. Fisk P.*	
" Mrs. Julia (Richards)*	
" Helen R. - - -	Sutton, Nebraska
" Mary E. - - - -	Sivas, Turkey
" Grace Lyman - - -	Grinnell, Iowa
" William Fisk - - -	Bozeman, Montana
" Albert David . - -	Grinnell, Iowa
Bray, Mrs. Mary E. - - -	Honolulu, Oahu
Brewer, Margaret A. - - -	New York City
Brigman, Mrs. Annie (Nott) -	Oakland, Cal
Brown, Chas. A. - . - -	Worcester, Mass
" Mrs. Irene (Ii) - -	Honolulu, Oahu
" George Ii - - .	" "
" Francis Hyde - - -	" "
Brown, Louisa J. *p* - - -	New York City
Brown, Mrs. M. Ella (Spooner) -	Northwood Center, N. H.
Burke. Mrs. Caroline (Frear)	
Butterworth, Joseph*	
Campbell, Elizabeth - - -	Honolulu, Oahu
Carpenter, Helen E. - - -	West Woodstock, Conn
Carter, Henry A. *p**	
" Mrs. Sybil Augusta (Judd)	Honolulu, Oahu
" Sybil Augusta*	
" Cordelia Judd - - -	..
" Joshua Dickson*	
Carter, Charles Lunt*	
" Henry A. P. - - -	Traveling in Europe
" Grace Stevens - - -	' "
Carter, George Robert - -	Honolulu, Oahu
" Mrs. Elizabeth - -	" "
Carter, Charlotte A. - - -	" "
" Mary N. - - - -	
" Joseph O., Jr. - - -	
Carter, Sarah M. - - - .	" "
Carter, Mrs. Edith M (Hartwell)	
Castle, Charles Alfred*	
Castle, Mary Eloise - - -	Chicago, Ill
" Hattie Ethelwin - -	" "
Castle, William Richards - -	Honolulu, Oahu
" Mrs. Ida B. (Lowrey) -	" "
" Wm. R., Jr.	Harvard University, Cambridge, Mass

* Deceased. *p* Photograph.

" Alfred Lowrey- - -	Honolulu, Oahu
" Alice Maud Beatrice -	" "
Castle, George P. - - -	" "
" Mrs. Ida M. (Tenney) -	
" Mary Hawley - - -	·· ··
" Margaret Tenney - -	" "
Castle, Caroline Dickenson - -	
Castle, Henry N.*	
" Mrs. Frida (Steckner)*	
" Helen Dorothy*	
" Mrs. Mabel (Wing) -	" - ··
" Eleanor Henry - -	
Castle, James B. - - -	
" Mrs. Julia (White) - -	
" Harold Long - - -	" "
Cathcart, Lillie - - - -	King Mt., N C
Chamberlain, Warren _p_ - -	Honolulu, Oahu
" Mrs. Celia (Wright)	" "
" Alethea M.*	
" Henry H.*	
Chamberlain, Horace W. - -	Chicago, Ill
" William Warren -	" "
Chamberlain, J. Evarts*ı	
Chamberlain, Martha A. J. - -	Honolulu, Oahu
Chamberlain, Rev. James P. -	La Crosse, Wis
" Mrs. Helen (Lightbody)	" "
" John Evarts - -	Mt. Vernon, Oregon
Chamberlain, Levi T. - - -	Honolulu, Oahu
Chapin, Elizabeth D. _p_ - -	Winchester, Mass
Church, Edward P. _p_ - -	Lansing, Mich
" Mrs. Frances L. - -	" "
Clark, Alvah R - - - -	Oakland, Cal
Clark, Mrs. Harriet E.*	
" Mary H.*	
" Arthur*	
Clark, Chas. K. - - - -	Berkeley, Cal
Clark, Mrs. Harriet (Howell) -	" "
" Fred Howell - - -	" "
Clark, Albert B., D.D.S. - -	Evanston, Ill
" Mrs. Sarah (Hamlin) -	" "
" Katalena H. - - -	" "
" Abbott Kittredge - -	
Clark, Prof. Wm. S.*	
" Mrs. Harriet (Richards) -	Newton, Mass
Clark, Mrs. Harriet M. (Gulick) -	Myazaki, Japan
" Admont Halsey - -	" "

---

* Deceased, _p_ Photograph

Coan, T. Munson, M.D., 70 Fifth Ave, New York City
Coan, Harriet F, *p*   -   -   -   Hilo, Hawaii
Coan, Latimer†
 "   Raymond Church   -   -   "   "
Coan, Mrs. Lydia (Bingham)   -   Honolulu, Oahu
Colcord, Chas. A.   -   -   -   Searsport, Maine
 "   Mrs. Lizzie E.   -   -   "   "
Coleman, Chas. C.   -   -   -
Coleman, Mrs. Harriet (Castle)   -
 "   Charles A. Castle*
 "   Samuel Northrop Castle   United States
Coleman, Horace Emery   -   -   Honolulu, Oahu
 "   Miss Floy (Rhode)   -   "   "
Conde, Rev. Samuel Lee   -   -   Rockford, Ill
 "   Pauline   -   -   -   -   "   "
 "   Charles A,   -   -   -   Philadelphia, Pa
 "   Henry T.   -   -   -   Indianapolis, Ind
 "   Mary *
Cooke, Joseph Platt* 4th
 "   Mrs. H- Emily (Wilder)   -   Oakland, Cal
 "   Grace M.   -   -   -   "   "
 "   William Gardner   -   -   "   "
 "   H. Ethelina*
Cooke, Joseph Platt 5th   -   -   Honolulu, Oahu
 "   Mrs. Maud (Baldwin)   -   "   "
 "   Joseph Platt 6th   -   -   "   "
 "   Emily Montague   -   -
Cooke, Charles Montague   -   -   "   "
 "   Mrs. Anna C. (Rice)   -   -   Oakland, Cal.
 "   Charles Montague, Jr.   -   "   "
 "   Wm. Harrison*
 "   George Paul   -   -   -
 "   Richard Alexander   -   -
 "   Alice Theodora   -   -
 "   Theodore Atherton   -   -   "   "
Cooke, Clarence Hyde   -   -   Honolulu, Oahu
 "   Mrs. Lily (Love)   -   -   "   "
Cooke, Amos Frank   -   -   -   "   "
 "   Mrs. Lillian (Lydgate)   -
 "   Margaret Montague   -   -
 "   Juliette Annis   .   -   -
Cooke, Clarence W.*
 "   Juliette M.   -   -   -   Minneapolis, Minn
Corbett, Mrs. Mary S. (Waterhouse)   Honolulu, Oahu
Corwin, John Howard   -   -   New York City
 "   Charles   -   -   -   -   Chicago, Ill

* Deceased. *p* Photograph. † Member of the Ladies' Society of Essex Street Church. Boston.

"   Cecil S. -   -   -   -   New York City
"   Arthur Mills, M.D.   -   Chicago, Ill
Cowperwaithe, Mrs. Clara (Pierpont)   Berkeley, Cal
Cox, Mrs. Lydia S. (Bean)   -   San Jose, Cal
Craft, Mrs. Helen K. (Wilder)   -   Honolulu, Oahu
Crawford, Mrs. Harriet J, (Sturges) *p*   Pomona, Cal
Crehore, Mrs. F. Isabelle (Carter)   Newton, Lower Falls, Mass
Crocker, Charles W. -   -   -   Chicago, Ill
"   Catherine   -   -   -   "   "
"   Mary W. (Moseley)*
"   Lillian Moseley   -   -
"   Charles -   -   -   "   "
Crockett, Mrs. Grace L. (Wing) -   Hamakua, Hawaii
Crozier, Mrs. Adelaide D, (Campbell)   Honolulu, Oahu
Cruzan, Edith   -   -   -   Berkeley, Cal
Cummings, Mrs. M. E. (Eckley) -   "   "
Damon, Samuel Mills -   -   -   Honolulu, Oahu
"   Mrs. Harriet M. (Baldwin)   "   "
"   Samuel Edward   -   -   "   "
"   May Mills   -   -   -
"   Henry Fowler   -   -
"   Douglas Wilfrid   -   -
Damon, Edward C.*
"   Mrs. Cornelia (Beckwith)
"   Fred Beckwith   -   -   "   "
"   William Francis   -   -   Lawrenceville, N J
"   Maurice Sherman -   -   "
"   Ethel Mosely -   -   -   Honolulu, Oahu
"   Julia Mills   -   -   -   "   "
Damon, Frank Williams   -   -   "   "
"   Mrs. Mary (Happer)   -
Damon, William F.*
Davis, Mrs. Isabelle (Lyons)   -   "   "
Dawson, Mrs. Bella (Martin)   -   Honoapu, Hawaii
Day, Mrs Julia H. (Lyman)   -   Aurora, Ill
De La Vergne, George   -   -   Honolulu, Oahu
"   Emily (Rice)   -   "   "
"   George Henry   -   Los Angeles, Cal
De La Vergne, Paul Findley   -   Honolulu, Oahu
"   Mrs. Clara (Kennedy)   "   "
Deacon, Henry -   -   -   -   Pepeekeo, Hawaii
"   Mrs. Kate (Wetmore)   -   "   "
"   Charles W.   -   -   -   Oakland, Cal.
"   Clyde -   -   -   -   Pepeekeo, Hawaii
"   Sheldon -   -   -   -   "   "
Deming, Mrs. Carrie (Rogers)   -   West Liberty, Iowa

---

* Deceased.   *p* Photograph

Dibble, Seymour H.*
Dickey, Charles Henry - - Haiku, Maui
  "   Mrs. Annie (Alexander) -   "   "
  "   Lyle Alexander - - Honolulu, Oahu
Dickey, Mrs. Frances, (Kinney) -   "   "
Dickson, Joshua G.*
  "   Mrs. Laura (Judd)* *p*
Dickson, Joshua Bates - - - Petaluma, Cal
Dickson, Mrs. Susan (Conde) - ? ——
Dillingham, Benjamin F. - - Honolulu, Oahu
  "   Mrs. Emma (Smith) -   "   "
Dillingham, Charles Augustus*
  "   Walter Francis - Cambridge, Mass
  "   Alfred H.*
    Harold Garfield - Berkeley, Cal.
  "   Marion Eleanor - Wellesley, Mass
Dillingham, Charles T.*
  "   Frank Thompson - Worcester, Mass
Dimond, William Henry*
  "   Mrs. Ellen (Waterhouse)*
  "   Mrs. Nellie (Gray)*
  "   Edwin R. - - San Francisco, Cal
Dimond, Edwin Hall - - - Honolulu, Oahu
Dimond, William Waterhouse - "   "
  "   Mrs. Carrie (Higby) - San Francisco, Cal.
Dodge, E. Stuart - - New York City
  "   Mrs. E. S. (Boyd)*
Dole, George H. - - - - Riverside, Cal
  "   Mrs. Clara (Rowell) - - "   "
  "   Walter Sanford - - - Honolulu, Oahu
  "   William Herbert - - - New York City
  "   Marion Foster - - - Riverside, Cal
  "   Clara Marie - - - "   "
Dole, Sanford Ballard - - Honolulu, Oahu
  "   Mrs. Anna P. (Cate) - - "   "
Dole, Mary - - - - Hallowell, Me
Doane, Edward W. - - Los Angeles, Cal
Drum, Mrs. Mary (Pierpont) - San Luis, Cal
Edwards, Mrs. Mary (Haven) - San Jose, Cal
Eels, James, Jr. - - - - Cincinnati, Ohio
  "   Emma L. A. - - - "   "
  "   Howard P. - - - "   "
  "   Emma P. - - -
  "   Stillman M. - - - "   "
Ellis, Francis E.† - - - Boston, Mass
Ellis, Hattie*

---

* Deceased. *p* Photograph.

Emerson, Samuel Newell - .	Honolulu, Oahu	
Emerson, Nathaniel Bright, M. D.	" "	
" Mrs. Sarah (Pierce) M. D.	" "	
" Arthur Webster - -	" "	
Emerson, Justin Edwards, M. D.	128 Henry St., Detroit	
" Mrs. W. H. (Elliot) M. D.	" "	
" Paul Elliot - - -	" "	
" Philip Law - - -		
" Ralph Pomeroy - -	" "	
Emerson, Joseph Swift - -	Honolulu, Oahu	
" Mrs. Dorothea (Lamb) -	" "	
Emerson, Rev. Oliver Pomeroy -	" "	
" Mrs. Eugenie (Homer) -	" "	
Farley, Mrs. Helen (Judd) - -	Auburndale, Mass	
" Ruth - - - -	" "	
" Emily - - - -	" "	
" Charles Judd - - -		
Farley, Mrs. Juliette (Smith) -		
Ferreira, Mary - - - -	Honolulu, Oahu	
Flaxman, Margaret - - -	" "	
" Sarah - - - -	" "	
Forbes, Rev. Anderson Oliver*		
" Mrs. Maria J. (Chamberlain)		
" Maria Rebecca - -		
" William Joseph - -	..	
" Harriet Gordon - -		
" Annie Isabella - -	" "	
Forbes, Agnes Boyd - - -	West Winsted, Conn	
Forbes, Major William T.*		
Forbes, Lieut. Theodore F. - -	Fort McPherson, Ga.	
" Theodore Frederick -	" "	
Frear, Rev. Walter p - - -	East Oakland, Cal	
" Mrs. Francis E. p	" "	
" Hugo P. p - -	San Francisco, Cal	
" Henrietta - - - -	East Oakland, Cal	
" Philip F. - - - -	Honolulu, Oahu	
Frear, Walter Francis - - -	Honolulu, Oahu	
" Mrs. Mary Emma (Dillingham)	" "	
Fuller, Robert M. - - -	" "	
" Ellen E. - - -	Oakland, Cal	
Furneaux, Charles - - -	Hilo, Hawaii	
Fyfe, Mrs. Julia (Johnson) - -	Petaluma, Cal.	
" Pauline D*		
" David K., Jr. - - -	" "	
Galt, Mrs. Agnes (Carter) - -	Honolulu, Oahu	
" John Randolph - - -	" "	

---

* Deceased. p Photograph.

Gamwell, Mrs. Elizabeth M.*
" Louise C. - - - Providence, R. I.
" Lauriston - - - " "
Gartley, Mrs. Ada (Jones) - - Philadelphia, Pa.
Gay, Mrs. Mary E. (Richardson)*
Gay, Mrs. Marion E. (Rowell) - Craftonville, Cal
Gilman, Mrs. Sarah - - - Honolulu, Oahu
" Caroline A. - - - Kirksville, Mo.
Gilman, Joseph A. - - - Honolulu, Oahu
" Mrs. Minnie (Brown) - " "
" Joseph Atherton - - " "
" Cordelia A. - - - ..
Goodale, Warren*
" Mrs. Ellen R.*
Goodale, Mary E. - - - Marlboro, Mass
" Charles W. - - - Butte City, Montana
Goodale, William W. - - - Waialua Plantation, Oahu
" Mrs. Emma M. (Whitney) " "
" Catherine Warren - - " "
" David Whitney*
Goodale, David - - - - Butte City, Montana
Goodrich, Charles B.*
Green, Mrs. Harriet (Parker) - Honolulu, Oahu
Green, Mary Elizabeth - W.C.T.U. Miss., Honolulu, Oahu
Green, Laura C. - - - Worcester, Mass
Green, A. T. - - - San Francisco, Cal
Green, Mrs. Mary (Paris) - - " "
" John Paris - - - " "
" Charles T. - - - " "
Green, Frank C. - - - - Worcester, Mass
Greer, Mrs. Helen C. (Lyman) - Chicago, Ill
Gulick, Rev. Luther Halsey*
" Mrs. Louisa (Lewis)*
" Kate*
" Edward Lacy - - - Lawrenceville, N. Y.
" Mrs. Harriet (Farnsworth) " "
" Leads - - - - " "
" Helen Farnsworth - -
" Caroline Elizabeth - -
" Pierre Johnson*
Gulick, Rev. Orramel H. - - Honolulu, Oahu
" Mrs. Ann Eliza (Clark) *p* " "
" Orramel H., Jr.*
" Paul Adams - - - Oberlin, Ohio
" Katherine P. - - - Cincinnati, Ohio
Gulick, Rev. John T. - - - Osaka, Japan

---

* Deceased. *p* Photograph.

"	Mrs. Emily*			
"	Mrs. Frances (Stevens)			
"	Addison	- - -	-	Oberlin, Ohio
',	Louise	- - -	-	" "
Gulick, Charles F.*				
Gulick, Rev. Wm. H	- -	-	Biarritz, France
"	Mrs. Alice (Gordon)	-	" "
"	James Gordon	- -	-	Cambridge, Mass
"	Frederic Carlton	- -	" "
"	Arthur Thomas*			
"	Bessie Marion	- -	-	Wellesley, Mass
"	Alice Gordon*	.		
"	Grace	- - -	-	Greenwich, Conn
Gulick, Theodore W.	- -	-	New York City
"	Mrs. Agnes (Thompson)	-	"
"	Walter Vose	- -	-	Chicago, Ill
"	James	- - -	-	Oberlin, Ohio
Gulick, Rev. Thomas L.	-	-	Devon, Pa
"	Mrs. Alice (Walbridge) p	"
Gulick, Julia Ann E. p	-	-	Traveling in U. S.
Gulick, Rev. Sidney Lewis	-	-	Shikokū, Japan
"	Mrs. Clara M. (Fisher)	-	"
"	Susan Fisher	- -	-	"
"	Luther Halsey	-	-	"
Gulick, Luther H., Jr.	-	-	Springfield, Mass
"	Mrs. Charlotte (Vetter)	-	" "
Gulick, Charles T.*				
"	Mrs. Sarepta A.	-	-	Honolulu. Oahu
Hair, Mrs. C. Amelia (Beckwith)	-	Hamakuapoko, Maui
Hall, Caroline A.*				
Hall, William W.	- -	-	Honolulu, Oahu
"	Mrs. Elizabeth (Van Cleve)p	" "
"	William Sibley*			
"	Horace Van Cleve p *		
"	Charlotte Van Cleve	-	-	Honolulu, Cal
. "	Theodore Seymour	-	-	Berkeley, Oahu
"	Edwin Oscar 2nd	-	-.	Honolulu, Oahu
"	Florence	- -	-	" "
"	Philip Cushman	-	-	" "
Hall, Mrs. Mary (Dame)	-	-	New York City
Hardy, Jacob	- -	-	Koloa, Kauai
"	Mrs. Elizabeth (Andrews)*		
"	Walter A.	- -	-	Hilo, Hawaii
"	Mary H.*			
"	William	- -	-	Hana, Maui
Hartwell, Alfred Stedman	-	-	Honolulu, Oahu

* Deceased. p Photograph.

"   Mrs. Charlotte E. (Smith)
,'   Charlotte Lee   -   -   Honolulu, Oahu
"   Juliette   -   -   -   "   "
"   Charles Atherton -   -   Cambridge, Mass
"   Bernice Dorothy   -   -   Honolulu, Oahu
Hartwell, Mrs. Mabel (Hartwell) -   Boston, Mass
Harvey, Mrs. Mary (Tinker)   -   Denver, Col
Harvey, Edna   -   -   -   -   Bangor, Maine
Hawkes, Mrs. Susan (Hyde)   -   Greenfield, Mass
"   William Hyde   -   -   "   "
Herring, Mary B.*
Hewitt, Mrs. Emma (Martin)   -   Waiohinu, Hawaii
Heydon, Edwin A.*
"   Edwin*
"   Asa Thurston -   -   -   Circle City, Alaska
"   Mary*
Higgins, Rev. John H.   -   -   Charleston, Me
"   Mrs. Ellen (H) McCully)   .   "
Hillebrand, Hermann*   .
"   Mrs. Elizabeth (Bishop)   New York City
"   Helen L   -   -   -   "
Hitchcock, D. Howard   -   -   Honolulu, Oahu
"   . Mrs. Hessie (Dickson)   "   "
Hitchcock, Charles Wetmore   -   Hilo, Hawaii
Hitchcock, Mrs. Alice (Hardy)*
"   Margaret   -   -   -   San Francisco, Cal
Hitchcock, Edward G.*
"   Mrs. Mary T. (Castle)   Hilo, Hawaii
"   Hattie C.   -   -   -   "
"   Edward N.   -   -   "
Hitchcock, Harvey Rexford -   .   -   Honolulu, Oahu
"   Mrs. Hannah J. (Meyers)   "   "
"   Harvey Rexford, Jr.   -   "   "
"   Randolph Howard   -
"   William Charles   -
Hobron, Mrs. Anna (Kinney)   -   "   "
Holman, Thomas S.   -   -   -   St. Paul, Minn
Holmes, Samuel*
"   Mrs. (Mary Goodale)   -   Montclair, N J
"   Mary Goodale   -   -   Los Angeles, Cal
"   David Goodale   -   Montclair, N J
"   George Day -   -   -   Chicago, Ill
"   Warren Goodale   -   '   -   Montclair, N J
Holmes, Samuel Judd -   -   -   "
"   Mrs. Josephine (Bautigam)   "
Hooker, Mrs. Martha V.* *p*

---

* Deceased.   *p* Photograph.

Hopper, Susan V.	Williamstown, Mass
Hopper, Margaret L.	Honolulu, Oahu
" Bessie Templeton	" "
Hosmer, Frank Alvin	Oahu College
" Mrs. Esther (Kellogg)	"
Houston, John A.	Gilman, Iowa
Houston, Albert Rhea	"
" Harold Danskin	"
Howard, Mrs. Hester L. (Dickson)	Los Angeles Cal
Howard, Albert S.	Townsend, Mass
" Mrs. Ellen (Goodale)	" "
Howard, Lewis Warren	" "
" David Goodale	" "
Howard, Walter Lincoln	Honolulu, Oahu
" Mrs. Margaret (Hare)	" "
Hustace, Anne	" "
Hyde, Rev. Charles M., D.D.	Honolulu, Oahu
" Mrs. Mary (Knight)	"
" Charles K.	Hilo, Hawaii
Hyde, Hon. William*	
" Mrs. Harriet (Sage)	Ware, Mass
" Harriet	"
Hyde, William S.	"
" Mrs. Elizabeth (Pitt)	
" Bessie*	
" Sylvia Sage	
Hyde, Henry K.	
" Mrs. Lucy R. (Hyde)	
" Ruth	"
Imhoff, Mrs. Haina (Aswan)	Honolulu, Oahu
Inch, Mrs. Clara M. (Dibble)	Washington, D C
Ingraham, Lucretia F.*	.
Isenberg, Paul	Bremen, Germany
" Mrs. H. Maria (Rice)*	
Isenberg, Paul R.	Waialae, Oahu
Isenberg, Mrs. Beta (Glade)	Bremen, Germany
" H. Alexander	Honolulu, Oahu
" Johannes Carl	Bremen, Germany
" Clara	"
" Richard	"
" Paulae	
Isenberg, Rev. Hans	
" Mrs. Dora (Isenberg)	"
Ives, Mrs. Helen (Chamberlain)	Pecatonica, Ill
Jarboe, Mrs. Eleanor (Dimond)	San Francisco, Cal
Jewett, Mrs. S. Fannie (Gulick)	Oberlin, Ohio

*Deceased.

Job, Mrs. Daniel O.† - · ·	South Walpole, Mass
Johnson, A. Frances - · ·	Ewa, Oahu
" Ellen A - · ·	"
Johnson, Henry - · ·	Petaluma, Cal
" Mrs. I. (Holden)*	
Jones, Peter Cushman - · ·	Honolulu, Oahu
" Mrs. Cornelia (Hall) - ·	" "
" Alice Hall - ·	Smith Col., Northampton, Mass
Jones, Edwin Austin* ᵃ	
" Mrs. Isabelle (Fuller) - ·	Honolulu, Oahu
" Edwin Austin, Jr.ᶦ - ·	" "
" Helen - · · ·	" "
" Margaret - · · ·	
" Catherine Hay - · ·	"
Jones, John J. - · · · ·	ᵣ Maui
Judd, Miss Harriet B.*	
Judd, Helen S. - · · ·	Honolulu, Oahu
Judd, Charles Hastings*	
" Mrs. Emily (Cutts) - ·	" "
" Emily Pauahi - · ·	New York City
Judd, Charles Hastings, 2nd ·	Honolulu, Oahu
" Charles Hastings, 3rd ·	" "
Judd, Albert Francis, L.L.D. ·	Honolulu, Oahu
" Mrs. Agnes (Boyd) - ·	" "
" Agnes Elizabeth - ·	" "
" James Robert - · ·	New York City
" Allen Wilkes - · ·	New Haven, Conn
" Henry Pratt - · ·	"
" Charles Sheldon - · ·	Honolulu, Oahu
" Sophia Boyd - · ·	" "
" Gerritt Parmelee - ·	" "
" Lawrence McCully - ·	
Judd, Allan W.*	
Judd, Albert Francis, Jr. - ·	"
" Mrs. Madeline (Hartwell) -	"ᶜ
Judd, Juliet I.*	
Kauhane, Mrs. Sarah (Martin) -	Kau, Hawaii
Kelly, Mrs. H. B. (Whitney) -	Honolulu, Oahu
Kelley, Kate - · · ·	" "
Kenyon, Miss M. F. - · ·	?
Kilborne, Mrs. Luella (Andrews)	E. Orange, N J
Kimball, Mrs. M. A. (Manross) -	Orange, Mass
King, Sara L - · · ·	San Francisco, Cal
King, Mrs. Lucy (Conde) - ·	Rockford, Ill
Kinney, Henry A.* ₚ	
Kinney, Harriet S.*	

---

*Deceased. † Member of Ladies' Society of Essex Street Church, Boston.

Kinney, Mrs. Sarah (Dimond)*
   "   Edward H. - · -   -   Humbrest, Iowa
   "   Henry R.*
   "   Jesse*
Kittredge, Dr. Charles S. -   -   Berkeley, Cal
   "   Mrs. Maria (C ase) -   "
   "   Rose Frances -   -   "
   "   Maud Chase -   "
   "   Mary Dame -   -   -   Wellesley, Mass
Kluegel, Mrs. Mary (Taylor) -   Honolulu, Oahu
Knight, Miss Eunice B.*
Kofoid, Mrs. Prudence (Winter) -   Urbana. Ill
Lawrence, Frances E. -   -   -   Honolulu, Oahu
Leadingham, Rev John -   -   "   "
   "   Mrs. Anna (Rich) -   ·'   '
Lewers, William Henry -   -   "   "
Lewis, Charles S.   -   -   -   Oakland, Cal
   "   Mrs. Lucy (Wetmore) -   "
   "   Raymond Whitin*
Lewis, Rev. John Morgan -   -   Wailuku, Maui
Leavitt, Mrs. Mary Clement‡   -   Boston, Mass
Leete, Hattie C. -   -   -   Guilford, Conn
Lillibridge, Mrs. Esther (Lyman) -   Akron, Iowa
Little, Mrs. S. C.   -   -   -   Oberlin, Ohio
Livermore, Mrs. Helen (Eels) -   Oakland, Cal
Locke, Mrs. Mary A. -   -   -   ?   Mass
Logan, Arthur C.   -   -   -   Buffalo, N Y
   "   Beulah -   -   -   Ruk, Micronesia
Lowrey, Fred J. -   -   -   Honolulu, Oahu
   "   Mrs. Cherry (Storrs) -   "   "
   "   Fred Dwight -   -   "   "
   "   Sherwood Moore -   -
   "   Helen Storrs -   -   -
   "   Allan Jewett -   "   "
Loebenstein, Mrs. Ella (Hitchcock)   Hilo, Hawaii
Ludlow, Helen W.   -   -   -   Hampton, Va.
Lydgate, Rev. John Mortimer -   Lihue, Kauai
Lyman, Dr. Henry M.   -   Chicago, Ill
   "   Mrs. Sarah (Clark) -   -   "
   "   Mary Isabella   `-   :   "
   "   Margaret K. -   -   -   Wellesley, Msss
   "   Henry M. Clark*
Lyman, Frederick S. -   -   -   Hilo, Hawaii
   "   Mrs. Isabella (Chamberlain)   "
   "   Ellen G.   -   -   -   Hilo Boarding School
   "   Frederick S., Jr. -   -   Honolulu, Oahu

---

* Deceased.   ‡ W. C. T, U. Missionary.

"	Francis Anderson, M.D.	Madison, Wis
"	Ernest E. - - -	Honolulu, Oahu
Lyman,	Levi C. - - - -	Hilo Boarding School
"	Mrs. Ncttie (Hammond)·	"
Lyman,	David Brainard, 2nd -	La Grange, Ill
"	Mrs. Mary (Cossitt)- -	"
"	David Brainard, 3rd -	"
"	Frank Cossitt*	
"	Mary Ellen - - -	
"	Paul Henry*	
Lyman,	Rufus Anderson - -	Hilo, Hawaii
"	Mrs. R. (Brickwood) -	"
"	Lilian H.*	
"	Rufus A. Jr. - - -	
··	Arthur B. K.*	
"	Henry J. - - -	Puna, Hawaii
"	Richard L. - · -	"
"	Eugene Hollis - -	Hilo, Hawaii
"	Norman K. - - -	"
"	David B. K. - . - -	Honolulu, Oahu
"	Muriel C. H.*	
"	Sarah Irene B. - -	Hilo, Hawaii
"	Clarence R. - - -	"
"	Albert K. - - -	"
"	Charles R. Bishop - -	
Lyman,	Ellen E.*	
Lyman,	Francis O. - ·- -	Chicago, Ill
"	Mrs. Charlotte (Dana) -	"
"	Ruth C *	
Lyons,	Curtis J. - - -	Honolulu, Oahu
"	Mrs. Julie E. (Vernon) -	" "
"	Emma F. -	" "
Lyons,	Fidelia M. - - -	Waimea, Hawaii
"	Elizabeth W.	" "
Lyons,	Dr. Albert B. - -	Detroit, Mich
"	Mrs Edith (Eddy)	" "
"	Edith Lucia - - -	" "
"	Albert Eddy - - -	" "
Mackenzie,	Rev. Robert - -	San Francisco, Cal
"	Mrs. Robert - -	" "
Mahelona,	Mrs. Susan (Kekela) ·	Ewa, Oahu
Malone,	Miss Nancy J. - -	Akron, Ohio
Mann,	Mrs. Sophia (Emerson)*	
Martin,	George H., M. D. -	San Francisco, Cal
Martin,	Mrs. Maria (Kekela) -	Waiohinu, Kau
Marques,	Mrs. Laura (Pires) -	Honolulu, Oahu

---

* Deceased.

McCall, Mrs. Emily (Whitney)*
"   Carrie E.   -   -   -   Saybrook, Conn
"   Henrietta W.*
McCoy, Henry J.   -   -   -   San Francisco, Cal
McCully, Lawrence*
"   Alice Lawrence   -   -   Charleston, Maine
McCully, Rev. Charles G.   -   -   Calais, Me
"   Mrs. Charles G.   -   -   "
"   Emma Lawrence -   -   "
"   Mary Porter*
McCully, Anna   -   -   -   Tokio, Japan
McLennan, Martha   -   -   -   New Cumberland, West Vir
Mead, George Herbert   -   -   Chicago University
"   Mrs. Helen (Castle)   -   -   "
"   Henry Albert   -   -   "
Meredith, Mrs. R· R.† -   -   .   Brooklyn, N Y
Merritt, Rev. Wm. C· -   -   -   Tacoma, Wash
"   Mrs. Marie (Dickenson)   -   "
Mills, Mrs. Kate (Vose)   -   -   Belfast, Me
Mitchell, Mary L.   -   -   -   Boston, Mass
Moore, Mrs. Almeda (Hitchcock)*
Moore, Mrs Nellie (Lowrey)   -   Hilo, Hawaii
Montague, Emily B.   -   -   -   Honolnlu, Oahu
Morris, Mrs. Louise (Kinney)   -   Sonoma, Cal
Morris, Miss Mlnnie   -   -   United States
Morse, Mrs. Mary (Chamberlain)   Worcester, Mass
Mory, Mrs. Maria (Pitman)   -   Chicago, Ill
Moseley, Mrs. Sophia (Bingharn)*
"   Hiram Bingham   -   -   Denver, Col
Murdock, Mrs. Mary E. (Baldwin)   Ewa, Oahu
Neal, Robert, M.D.*
"   Mrs. Florence (Andrews) p *
Needham, Miss Hattie -   -   -   Honolulu, Oahu
Newell, Mrs. Margaret (Hardy)   -   San Francisco, Cal
Nichols. C Fessenden, M.D.   -   Boston, Mass
Norton, Helen S.   -   -   -   Howell, Mich
Nott, Mrs. Mary Ellen (Andrews)   Hammond, La
"   Sarah Thurston -   -   -   Oberlin, Ohio
"   Elizabeth W.   -   -   -   "
"   Mary Andrews   -   -   -   Hammond, La
Nott, Mrs. Laura Dickson) -   -   New York City
Oleson, Rev. Wm. B.   -   -   -   Worcester, Mass
"   Charles Merwin*
"   Edward Prince   -   -   "
"   Mary Hall   -   -   -

---

* Deceased.   p Photograph.   † Member of the Ladies' Society of Essex Street Church. Boston.

"   David Lyman ·   -   -
Page, Simon*
Palmer, Rev. Frank H.   -   -   Boston, Mass·
"   Mrs. Lucy (White) *   ''
"   Herbert Hall ·   -   -   ''
"   Allison Cleveland ·   ·   ''
Park, Annie C.   ‧   ‧   -   -   Bennington, Vt
Parke, Jennie S. ·   -   -   -   Honolulu, Oahu
Parker, Rev. Henry H.   ‧   ‧   ''
Paris, Ella H.   -   ‧   -   -   Kona, Hawaii
Paris Anna ‧   -   -   -   Honolulu, Oahu
Paris, John D.   -   -   ‧   -   Kona, Hawaii
"   Mrs. Hannah (Johnson)   ‧   ''
"   Mary E.   -   -   ‧   -   Oakland, Cal
"   John Davis, Jr. ‧   -   Honolulu, Oahu
"   James Robert   -   ‧   ‧   ''
Parsons, Mrs Henry M *†
Paulding, Christina Wood   ‧   -   Prin. Kawaiahao Seminary
Payson, Adela M.   -   -   -   San Francisco, Cal
Pease, Edmund M., Jr.   -   -   Claremont, Cal
Perry, Charles F.   -   -   -   Kamehameha Manual Sch.
Perry, Rev. Silas P.   -   -   -   ''   · ''
"   Mrs Ellida (Oleson) ·   ‧   ''   ''
Pepoon, Helen C.   -   -   ‧   Painesville, Ohio
Pierce, Miss Harriet C.   ‧   -   Honolulu, Oahu
Pierce, Henry A.*
Pierson, Mary   ‧   ‧   ‧   -   Glen Rose, Texas
Pinder, Susan E. ·   -   -   -   Honolulu, Oahu
Pitman, T Henry*
"   Benjamin F. ·   -   -   Boston, Mass
Pogue, Rev. J F.*
"   Mrs. Maria (Whitney)   ‧   Santa Clara, Cal
"   Samuel W.   -   -   ‧   ''
"   Jane K.   ‧   -   ‧   ''
"   Emily E. ‧   ‧   -   ‧   ''
Pogue, William F.   -   -   -   Makawao, Maui
Pond, Percy. Martyn -   -   -   Honolulu, Oahu
Pope, Ida M.   -   -   -   Prin. Kamehameha Girls' School
Porte, de la, Philip Adam   ‧   -   Pleasant Is., Micronesia
Porte, de la, Mrs. Salome ‧   -   ''   ''
Porter, Mrs. Lily (Brewer) ·   -   Worthington, Minn
Potter, Susan M. ·   -   -   -   Port Jefferson, L I
Pratt, Mrs. Sophia H. (Boyd)   -   Honolulu, Oahu
Pratt, Amasa -   -   -   -   Columbus, Ohio
"   Mrs. Louise   -   ·   -   ··
Pratt, Lewellyn   -   -   -   ''

---

*Deceased. † Member of Ladies' Society of Essex Street Church, Boston.

" Mrs. Helen A. (Dickson) -	"
Pratt, Mrs. S. Catherine (Dickson)	Honolulu, Oahu
Pratt, Mrs. Abbie (Tinker) - -	Titusville, Pa
Rand, Mabel - - - -	Northfield, Mass
Renwick, Isabella - - -	Kohala, Hawaii
Reynolds, Mrs. Lucy (Bingham)*	
" Mary C. - - ´	St. Augustine, Fla
" Erskine H. - - -	"
" Kate L. - - -	"
Rice, William H.*	
" Mrs. Mary S. H. - - -	Lihue, Kauai
Rice, William Hyde, 2nd - -	Honolulu, Oahu
" Mrs. Mary (Waterhouse) -	"
" Charles Atwood - - -	Lihue, Kauai
" Arthur H. - - -	Stanford, Cal
" Mary Eleanor - - -	Honolulu, Oahu
" Anna Charlotte - - -	" "
" Harold Waterhouse - -	Lawrenceville. N J.
" Philip De La Vergnǝ - -	Honolulu, Oahu
Rice, William Henry 3rd - . -	Lihúe, Kauai
" Mrs. Mary Agnes (Girvin) -	"
Rice, Mary S. H.*	
Rice, Rev. W. H. - - -	Oberlin, Ohio
Richards, Dr. James A.*	
Richards, Helen C.*	
Richards, Theodore - - -	Honolulu, Oahu
" Mrs. Mary C. (Atherton)	"
" Ruth - - . -	"
" Joseph Atherton - -	
Riemenschneider, H.*	
" Mrs. Ellen (Rowell)p	Riverside, Cal
Ritz, Laura A. - - - -	Ohio ?
Robertson, Cornelia D. - -	Tacoma, Wash
Rogers, W. Harvey - -	Hilo, Hawaii
Rogers, Mrs. Malvina (Rowell)p *	
" Kate Lincoln - - -	Medford, Mass
" Edmund Horton - -	"
Rouse, Rev. Fred T. - -	Appleton, Wis
Rowell,· William Edwards - -	Honolulu, Oahu
" George A. - - -	Brooklyn, N Y
Sage, Sarah R. - - -	Ware, Mass
Sanford, Mrs. Lulu K. (Reynolds)	Rutherford, N J
Sayford, Samuel M. - - -	Newton-Corners, Mass
Schoen, Bertrand Ferdinand -	Hilo, Hawaii
" Mrs. Mabel (Hitchcock) -	"
" Evelyn Henrietta - -	"

* Deceased. p Photograph.

Schofield, Nathan - - -	Honolulu, Oahu
Scott, Mrs. H. A. *p* - - -	Hamilton, Ohio
Scott, Mrs. Emma (Clark) - -	Hilo Hawaii
" Irwin - - - -	"
" Margaret - - - -	"
' Alvah Allison - - -	"
Scudder, Mrs. David C.† - -	Brookline, Mass
Scudder. Jane M.† - - -	Boston, Mass
Searle, Susan A.† - - -	Kobe, Japan
Severance, Mrs. Lucinda (Clark) -	Hilo, Hawaii
" Helen - - -	"
" Allen Parke- - -	Barre, Mass
Severance, Rev. Claude Milton -	Cleveland, Ohio
Seymour, Theodore S. - - -	Milford, Iowa
" Mrs. Theodore S. - -	"
Shaw, Jonathan - - - -	Honolulu, Oahu
" Mrs. Delia (Bishop) - -	"
" Ruth Cornelia - - -	"
" Jessie Cunningham - -	
" Margaret Fenton - -	"
Shepard, Fred D. M.D. *p* - -	Aintab, Turkey
" Fanny (Andrews) *p* -	"
" Florence A. - - -	Philadelphia, Pa
" Alice Claudia - - -	"
Shipman. William H. - - -	Hilo, Hawaii
Shipman, Ollver Taylor - -	Olaa, Hawaii
Simpson, Lizzie W. - - -	Christianburg, Va
" Margaret D. - - -	"
" Dora - - - -	"
Simpson, Mrs. Helen J. (Kinney)-	Chicago, Ill
Sisson, Mrs. Ellen (Holden)*	
Small, Sallie B.*	
Smith, Augustus L.*	
" Mrs Clara (Benfield) -	Honolulu, Oahu
Smith, Emma C. - - - -	Pasadena, Cal
Smith, William Owen - - -	Honolulu, Oahu
" Mrs. Mary A. (Hobron) -	"
" Clarence Hobron . -	Cambridge, Mass
" Anna Kathrine - - -	Honolulu, Oahu
" Lorrin Knapp - - -	"
Smith, Jared K., M.D.*	
Smith, Alfred H. - - -	Lihue, Kauai
Smith, Mrs. Lucilla (Bates) - -	San Francisco, Cal
Smith, Mrs M. L. - - -	"
Smith, Frank Tallent - - -	"
Smith, Mrs Eloise T. (Hitchcock)	

---

* Deceased, *p* Photograph. † Member of the Ladies' Society, Essex Street Church, Boston.

Snow, Caroline - - - - Honolulu, Oahu
Snow, Fred Galen - - - Olaa Hawaii
" Mrs. Mary Rebecca (Hitchcock) "
Snow, Ella B. - - - - Honolulu, Oahu
Speer, John E. - - - - Philadeiphia, Penn
" James R. - - - - "
" Hetty M. - - - - "
Stangenwald, Hugo, M.D.*
" Mrs. Mary C. (Dimond)*
" William Hugo*
" Frank Dimond*
" Charles Gustave*
" Mrs Anna M. (Dimond) Honolulu, Oahu
Stetson, Mrs. A. H.†*
Stevenson, Mrs. Alice (Thurston) - Taylorsville, N C
Stewart, Martha W.*
Stewart, Harriet B.*
Stewart, C. Seaforth, Colonel Retired U. S. A., Cooperstown, NY
" Mrs. C. S. p*
" Charles Seymour*
" Cecil - - - - U. S. Army
" Cora*
Stolz, Fred L. - - - - San Francisco, Cal
Stolz, Mrs. Mary A. (Rowell) M. D. Brooklyn, N Y
Street, Mrs. Mary (Anderson) p - Exeter, N H
Sturges, Ella M.*
Sturgeon, Mrs. Juliet M. (Sturgess) Los Angeles, Cal
Sunter, Mrs. Sarah (Rogers) - Kona, Hawaii
Sutherland, Louis L. - - Minneapolis, Minn
" Mrs. Clara L. (Moseley) " "
Sutherland, Mrs. Meta (Bruns) - Honolulu, Oahu
Swanzy, Mrs. Julia (Judd) - " "
" Geraldine F.*
Talbot, Mrs. Edith Hull (Armstrong) Boston, Mass
Tarbell, Mrs. Isabel (Ferreira) - Honolulu, Oahu
Taylor, Rev. Townsend E.*
" Mrs. Persis (Thurston) - " "
" George C.*
" Henry T. - - - Hilo, Hawaii
" James - - - - Honolulu, Oahu
" Edward Seaforth - - San Francisco, Cal
Taylor, Julia L. p - - - Kelloggsville, Ohio
Terry, Willard S. - - - Hilo, Hawaii
Thompson, Rev. Frank - - Valparaiso, Chili, S A
" Mrs. Louise - - " "
" Carrie L. H. p - - " "

---

*Deceased. p Photograph.

Thompson, Maria Dorothea *p* -
Thompson, Mark V. C.*
Thrum, Thomas G. - - - Honolulu, Oahu
" Mrs. Anna L. (Brown) - " "
Thurston, Asa G. *p* *
" Mrs. Sarah (Andrews)*
" Robert T. *p* *
Thurston, Lorrin Andrews -
" Mrs. M. Clara (Shipman)*
" Robert Shipman -
" Margaret Carter -
Thurston, Rev. Thomas G.*
" Mrs. Francis R.*
" Alice*
" Lucy G. - - - Taylorsville, N C
" Asa 3rd *p* - - - " "
Tobin, Mrs. Mary G. (Dimond) San Francisco, Cal
Tousley, Mrs. Sophia (Corwin)*
Townsend, Mrs. Cora (Hitchcock) Honolulu, Oahu
Tucker, Edwin W. - - - San Francisco, Cal
" Mrs. Jennie (Scott) - " "
Tucker, Joshua D. - - - Honolulu, Oahu
Tufts, Mrs. Arthur W. † - - Boston, Mass
Turner, M. Annis Montague (Cooke) Oakland, Cal
Turner, Charlotte L. - - Waihee, Maui
Van Cleve, Samuel H., M. D. - Minneapolis, Minn
" Paul L. - - - Billings, Mont
Van Duzee, Cyrene - - - New York
Van Slyke, Lawrence Prescott - Geneva, N Y
Walsh, Edward M. - - - Oakland, Cal
" Mrs Julia (Beckwith)*
" Marion Beckwith - - " "
" Maurice Edward - - " "
Warfield, F. A † - - - Omaha, Neb
Waterhouse, John T., Jr.*
" Mrs. Elizabeth (Pinder) Honolulu, Oahu
" Fred Thos. Pinder " "
" Ernest C. - - " "
Waterhouse, Henry " "
" Mrs. Julia (Dimond)*
" Henry, Jr. - -
" Frank*
" Albert - - - Lawrenceville, N J
Waterhouse, William - - Pasadena, Cal
" Mrs. Lena (Smith) - " "
" Alfred Herbert - Princeton, N J

---

* Deceased. *p* Photograph. † Member of the Ladies' Society of Essex Street Church, Boston.

"	Lawrence Hartwell	Pasadena, Cal
"	Paul Bernard -	" "
"	Gerald Condit -	" "
"	Milicent -	" "
Waters, Mrs. Sarah E. (Coan) -		New York City
Weaver, Philip Lewis - -		San Francisco, Cal
" Mrs. Ellen (Armstrong)		" "
" Clarice Chapman -		" "
Weddick, Mrs. Winifred (Baldwin)		Wailuku, Maui
Wells, Mrs. Mildred (Kinney) -		Honolulu, Oahu
West, Alice - - - -		Hilo, Oahu
Wetmore, Charles H. Jr.*		
Wetmore, Frances, M.D. - -		Hilo, Hawaii
Wetmore, Charles - - -		(Residence unknown)
White, Mrs S. (Hall) _p_ *		
White, Edwin Oscar - - -		Honolulu, Oahu
" Mrs. Ella (Street)*		
" Clifford F. - - -		"
White, Nellie M. - - -		" "
Whitman, Russell - - -		Oakland, Cal
Whitney, Rev. Samuel W. _p_ - -		Germantown, Pa
Whitney, Henry M. - - -		Honolulu, Oahu
Whitney, Mrs. Catherine (Marsh)*		
" Hervey E.*		
" Henry M., Jr. -		Honolulu, Oahu
" James N.*		
" Albert L.*		
" Frederick D *		
Whitney, John M., D.D.S. _p_ -		Honolulu, Oahu
" Mrs. Mary (Rice) - -		" "
" William Locke - -		New York City
" Ada Rice - - -		Honolulv, Oahu
Whitney, John Russell*		
" Edward Fiske - -		Eldred, N Y
Wight, Mrs. Laura (Wilder) - -		Honolulu, Oahu
Wilcox, Charles H.*		
" Mrs. Adelia (Van Meter) -		Oakland, Cal
" Ella L. - - - -		"
" Lucy Eliza - - -		"
" Charles H., Jr. - -		
" Norton Edward - -		"
Wilcox, George Norton - -		Lihue, Kauai
Wilcox, Albert Spencer - -		"
" Mrs. Emma N. (Mahelona)		"
Wilcox, Samuel W. - - -		
" Mrs. Emma (Lyman) -		

* Deceased. _p_ Photograph,

"   Ralph Lyman -   -   "
"   Lucy Etta   -   -   -   Wellesley, Mass
·'   Elsie Hart   -   -   -   "
"   Charles Henry   -   -   Oakland, Cal
"   Gaylord Parke   -   -   Andover, Mass
"   Mabel Isabel -   -   -   Oakland, Cal
Wilcox, Edward P.   -   -   -   West Winsted, Conn
"   Mrs. Mary (Rockwell)   -   "
Wilcox, W. Luther   -   -   Honolulu, Oahu
"   Clarence S.*
Wilcox, Henry H.*
"   Mrs. Mary T. (Green)   -   Honolulu, Oahu
Wilder, Mrs. Elizabeth Kinau (Judd)   "
"   William C.*
"   Gerrit P.   -   -   -   Honolulu, Oahu
"   Samuel G. Jr. -   -   -   "
"   James H.   -   -   -   Paris, France
Wilkinson, Mrs. Arthur†   -   -   Cambridge, Mass
Williams, George C.*
"   Mrs. S. Elizabeth (Johnson) Petaluma, Cal
Williams, Mrs. Eloise (Castle)   -   Honolulu, Oahu
Williston, Levi Lyman*
"   Mrs. Anna (Gale)   -   ·.
Winne, Mrs. Lucy (Taylor)   -
Wood, Arthur B.   -   -   -
"   Mrs. Eleanor (Waterhouse)   "
Woodward, Mrs Elizabeth (Frear)   Santa Rosa, Cal
Woodward, Mrs. Grace (Richards)   New York City
Wolfe, Mrs. Nina (Goodale)   -   Honolulu, Oahu
Wolters, Mrs. Julia (Isenberg)   -   Lihue, Kauai
Ziegler, Miss M. Ida -   -   -   Haiku, Maui
Zumwalt, Mrs. Mary (Bailey   -   Kahului, Maui

---

* Deceased. ℗ Photograph.

ANNUAL MEMBERS—1898–1899.

Andrews, Lorrin - - - - - Honolulu, Oahu
Coleman, Horace Emery - - - - "
Coleman, Mrs. Floy Rhode - - - - "
Dickey, Charles William - - - -
Kinney. Mrs. Selma S. - - - - - ..
"   Henry Walsworth - - - - ..
"   Maud Miriam - - - - -
Soares, Rev. A. V. - - - - -
"   Mrs. A. V. - - - - -
Weaver, Philip L. - - - - -

RECAPITULATION.

Honorary Members not of Hawaiian Mission—Living - 45
"   "   —Deceased 17
    —— 62

Life Members—Living - - - - - - - 946
"   Deceased - - - - - 200
    —— 1146

Annual Members - - - - - - - - 10
  ——
Total - - - - - - - - - 1208

OFFICERS

FOR 1898-9.

REV. J. LEADINGHAM, President.

REV. A. V. SOARES, Vice-President.

REV. O. H. GULICK, Recording Secretary.

MARTHA A. CHAMBERLAIN and CHARLOTTE V. C.
Corresponding Secretaries.

LYLE A. DICKEY, Treasurer.

JOS. S. EMERSON and MRS. L. B. COAN, Elective Me
of the Board.

OFFICERS

FOR 1899-1900.

A. FRANCIS COOKE, President.

FRANK C. ATHERTON, Vice-President.

LORRIN ANDREWS, Recording Secretary.

MARTHA A. CHAMBERLAIN and ADA R. WHITNEY,
Responding Secretaries.

LYLE A. DICKEY, Treasurer.

REV. J. LEADINGHAM and MRS. W. F. FREAR, Eli
Members of the Board.

CPSIA information can be obtained
at www.ICGtesting.com
Printed in the USA
BVHW040907281118
534010BV00038B/496/P